LITERACY FROM HOME TO SCHOOL
Reading with Alice

Robin Campbell

Trentham Books

First published in 1999 by Trentham Books Limited

Trentham Books Limited
Westview House
734 London Road
Oakhill
Stoke on Trent
Staffordshire
England ST4 5NP

British Cataloguing in Publication Data
A catalogue record for this book is available from the British Library
ISBN: ISBN 1 85856 166 3

Designed and typeset by Trentham Print Design Ltd, Chester and
printed in Great Britain by The Cromwell Press Ltd., Wiltshire

LITERACY FROM HOME TO SCHOOL
Reading with Alice

Contents

Acknowledgements

This book could not have been written without the wholehearted support of Robert and Susan. They agreed to my collecting information on their daughter Alice. Her progress as a reader and writer was observed in a number of literacy contexts. Most particularly I observed Alice reading books with significant adults in her life. Eventually Alice's younger sister Caitlin became part of the study as she shared books with Alice. By the end of the book Dylan put in an appearance and Alice was able to act as a guide for her brother's literacy development.

As ever, my wife Ruby reminded me of the connections to early years settings. She also questioned my writing and evaluated my comments. But this time she appears also as one of the adults guiding and supporting Alice through story books.

Once my ideas were on paper Gillian Klein provided an editorial role which ensured that the text said what I wanted it to say and not just what I thought it said.

Even so, this book could not have been written without Alice. Now some months after completing the text it is a delight to see her still enthusiastically engaged with reading and writing. I am very grateful to my granddaughter.

Chapter 1
Introduction

This is a story about Alice. And it is about the wonderland of print, books and reading that Alice entered during the first five years of her life before starting formal schooling. The story is told through a series of vignettes or snapshots of Alice's encounters with language and especially print – usually with the support of a significant adult. One of those significant adults, her paternal grandfather, is me. And collecting, and analysing, observations of young children learning to read (and then writing about it) was what I had been doing during much of my professional career.

The majority of my observation, analysis and writing about young children learning to read was based in primary classrooms, and it always took account of the fact that children came to school with knowledge about reading and in many cases were already reading. I have also considered the pre-school child sharing a book or reading with an adult (Campbell, 1995; 1996). However this book is concerned mainly with Alice reading before she began school.

How can a grandfather write objectively about a granddaughter? There are three immediate answers to this. First, remaining detached from literacy activities in order to write about them is what I had been doing before, even though at times I may have had to enforce that objectivity upon myself. Second, I present some of the interactions as transcripts, so you can make your own interpretations of the developments I describe. Third, there is a long history of parents reporting upon their children's literacy development and those texts have presented us with enough data for us to feel confident about the objectivity of the writing despite the close relationship between the child and the adult.

The study by Glenda Bissex (1980) of her son Paul learning to read and write is perhaps one of the most well known parent-child case studies. The numerous examples of Paul's writing development is a major feature, emphasised by the intriguing title of the book, *Gnys at Wrk*.

There were earlier studies: Dorothy White (1954) provided a diary of her daughter Carol engaging with a wide range of *Books Before Five*. That White was a librarian is reflected in the wealth of books that Carol had read to her during her first five years and which provided many play opportunities for Carol. That books did also for Lindsey and Ashley we can see in Shelby Wolf's (Wolf and Heath, 1992) account of her daughters' encounters with children's literature. The characters and plot of that literature could be observed in the play activities of the children, which suggests that story reading before schooling does even more than help children to learn to read.

Judith Schickedanz (1990) continued the tradition with her account of *Adam's Righting Revolution*. In her account, her son Adam develops as a writer in front of our eyes, because we have the examples of his writing and his mother's analysis to help us to see his development. And there are other parent-child accounts (for example Laminack (1991) and Martens (1996)), aspects of whose texts will appear later – among others.

That I pay little attention here to those stories of young children developing as readers and writers is not because they are not valuable but because this book is about Alice. So it is Alice who should have centre stage.

Alice shared books with the significant adults in her family and examples of those shared story readings forms the main focus of this book. Over five years the readings alter and develop, as the monthly samples of Alice reading with an adult demonstrate, as Alice learns about reading and how to read. Alice learns to read not because she is taught to read but because the literacy activities and experiences help her to construct her own understanding of reading and writing. The development of Alice as a reader will be of interest to early childhood teachers as well as to parents and other carers, since it provides further evidence of how young children can be guided and supported towards literacy.

Chapter 2
From Birth to One

Alice arrived in time for evening story time. But everyone involved in the birth, directly or indirectly, was too exhausted, excited and pre-occupied to give a thought to such a literacy activity. For the moment Alice, together with her mother, was enough.

Indeed, how soon would you want to start reading stories to a baby anyway. Surely not on the first day? Lester Laminack (1991), in *Learning with Zachary*, describes how he started telling stories to Zachary before birth and suggested that Zachary appeared to move or kick during story times. And David Doake (1988) includes in his book a picture of his son being read to by his mother at six hours of age. So when might story times begin? There is no precise answer. But the fact that the questions might be asked at all indicates that reading with Alice would be starting, in a range of ways, during the early months of her first year of life.

The first six weeks may seem an eternity to parents. Feeding, changing, cleaning and broken nights without sleep seem to be the major events of life. But Alice was growing and developing all the time. And she was being surrounded by literacy activities, some deliberate and others more incidental.

> Alice's father was reading a novel, but unexpectedly he was reading it out aloud. That was unexpected because we normally expect that adults will read novels silently to themselves. But on this occasion Alice was being cuddled on one arm while her father read the book aloud. (2 months)

We do not know what Alice will have gained from the activity but at the time it appeared to be the sensible thing to do for other reasons. Her father could read his book, Alice could be cuddled, reassured, and settled. Furthermore, although it was not the intention of the activity, words and books were becoming part of her everyday environment.

That parents read their own reading material aloud to a very young child may be more common than we realise. Julie Spreadbury (1994) reported that she and her husband read to their son Scott from newspapers, magazines and parts of books that were being studied at the time. These were not deliberate attempts to teach the young child but were incidental and inevitably of materials that the parent needed or wanted to read at the time. However, reading their own reading materials to their children lasts for only a short time.

Some time between six and eight weeks it became obvious that Alice was able to focus on objects, faces and her immediate environment. This meant that Alice now was able to focus on the adult or the book (but not the print in the book) and take in further meaning and understandings about literacy, albeit understandings that were tentative, incomplete and non-verbal. Nonetheless, Alice's new capability seemed to encourage the adults around her to read to her.

Furthermore, the non-verbal aspect was about to change, because Alice was producing sounds. And these sounds were increasingly used as part of an elementary conversation. When they spoke with Alice, adults used intonation and pauses to encourage Alice to take turns in the conversation. Only the adults used words but Alice responded with sounds, smiles, eye contact, arm movements and leg thrashing. It may have been the skills of the adults which made it look like a conversation with each party taking a turn. But it was part of a development which would lead in due course to real conversations and eventually to conversations which would be centred on a book.

By three months Alice would become excited when she had songs and rhymes sung to her. Her smiles, the sounds she made and the movements of her body, when her mother (M) or father (F) sang to her, indicated her involvement with and enjoyment of these events. A particular favourite became the family adaptation of the Tigger song from Walt Disney's film of Winnie the Pooh and the Blustery Day.

M   The wonderful thing about Alice
is Alice's a wonderful thing.
Her top is made out of rubber,
her bottom is made out of spring.
She's bouncy, bouncy, bouncy,
fun, fun, fun, fun, fun.
But the most wonderful thing about Alice is,
she's the only one.
She's the only one, prrrrr.
(3 months)

Within a few days Alice appeared to anticipate at least two parts of that song. The words, the rhyme, and/or the intonation led her to expect the gentle bounces that she would receive half-way through the song. Second, her facial expression seemed to indicate that she expected the flow of air, which her parents directed towards her cheek, during the 'prrrrr' at the end of the song. And, as we have come to expect of very young children, it is the adults who tire of the activity before the child. Young children love to repeat what they know and enjoy. So Alice welcomed the song time and time again.

We can only guess at what learning takes place in such circumstances. However, the fact that the event was centred on language, in this case a song, in a context of great enjoyment, surely means that some basis for language and literacy development was being established.

Other language interactions took place regularly and frequently during those early months. In particular Alice enjoyed her mother singing to her:

M   London's Burning, London's Burning.
Fetch the engine, fetch the engine.
Fire, fire. Fire, fire.
Pour on water, pour on water. (3 months)

Picture 1: Sharing a book with mother. 3 months

With her new-found ability to produce sounds, Alice took part in those singings though they were not distinguishable as words – and the sounds became louder and more frequent each day.

At this time Alice also began to enjoy her first book *My Favourite Things* (Early Learning Centre, n.d.). This cloth picture book of eight pages had very bright colours and it was this perhaps which so attracted Alice. As she grabbed at the book and moved the pages (it would be an exaggeration to call it 'turning the pages') she would also hear adults informing her about the pictures and including some of the language of books e.g.

F Look there's the rabbit.
  Can you see his big ears?
  I think he's going to eat that carrot
  Let's see what's on the next page shall we?
  What's this a picture of?
  (4 months)

Alice was being helped to understand that pictures can represent objects and events. She was also hearing, along with comments about the pictures, certain words with which she would need to become familiar as a literacy learner: picture, page, next etc. She would learn them not because they were directly taught but because they would be part of the language used during the regular and frequent contact with books.

Another favourite book of Alice's in these early months was the colourful Animal Board Book, *Big Animals* (Lyons, 1986). On each little page there is an illustration of an animal, except for the whale which gets the double page in the middle of the book. The illustrations are on a plain bright background which is attractive but does not distract from the picture. Under each picture is written the name of the animal. So whenever an adult shared this book with Alice, probably two or three times every day, Alice would see the pictures, hear the name of the animal and get various descriptions of the animals.

Grandmother (Gm) There's the Chimpanzee
And over on the other page is the Kangaroo.
The kangaroo goes hop, hop, hop, doesn't it?
(5 months)

Alice would sometimes be given the book to hold. She could not yet hold and turn pages so she would just hold and look at whichever page was open. Or rather, stare intently, because that was certainly the impression that she gave. But Alice was teething and anything within her grasp would eventually reach her mouth and be pressed between her gums. It would take time for her to learn how to treat books but the early books were of cloth or board and reasonably able to stand up to such treatment.

Each day brought different interests and growth. So for a few days her main interest and activity would be staring intently at objects, people and events – relatively silently. During those days the use of sounds was somewhat infrequent. Then for a few days came the babbling which appeared to preoccupy Alice's waking hours almost constantly from very early in the morning until she fell asleep at night.

Alice enjoyed the games and activities with her parents, especially when these involved movement – and which included incidentally the language of nursery rhymes.

M   See-saw Marjorie Daw
Alice shall have a new master
She shall have but a penny a day
because she can't go any faster.
(6 months)

It did not take more than a few see-saws on the knees of her mother, father or one of her grandparents, before Alice demonstrated that she was anticipating the faster movement of the see-saw in the last line of the nursery rhyme, indicating her growing understanding of language as well as her memory of the event and the sequence within it. Alice's anticipation of the final episode in language games was also apparent when she watched the finger route of the 'Teddy Bear' around the palm of her hand and then up her arm in three short steps:

Gm   Round and round the garden
Went the Teddy Bear,
One step,
Two steps,
Tickle under there.
(7 months)

As time went by, Alice was prepared to accept a longer and longer pause after the second step before the tickle. And during this pause she would look intently at the finger resting by her elbow. She was able to predict the next step and thus anticipate the funny ending. (This well-known language game is one of many that parents can play with their babies. Texts such as *This Little Puffin .... Finger Plays and Nursery Games* compiled by Elizabeth Matterson (1969) provide numerous examples.

Her physical response and eye movements to calls of 'Alice' suggested that some words were now invested with meaning for her, most particulary her name. Young children learn their names in the spoken form very early in their language development and they typically replicate that interest when they begin to write letters and words some months later. The child's name is often the first recognisable word in their scribbles/writing.

Although the cloth and board books, with their simple pictures of objects, continued to attract Alice's attention, she was also introduced to some of the short picture books with a central character. Jill Bennett (1991) observed that Spot the dog was 'probably the most well known and best-loved picture-book character of recent times' (p11) and Alice reacted with interest to *Spot's first words* (Hill, 1966), looking at the pictures and listening to the words rather than trying to bite on the book.

Grandfather (Gf) There's Spot sitting on a chair.

And he's reading a book.
There he is.
> *Spot looks inside a box and finds a*

Can you see what he found?
> *a toy car.*

Then
> *Spot takes a book to read in his chair.*

(7 months)

Alice was able to listen to the words of the book but she was also given a commentary and invited to participate in the story reading – 'Can you see what he found?' At this stage her contribution remained physical and non-verbal, although she did babble at the book.

Over the next few weeks *Spot's first words* gave Alice ever-increasing pleasure. For instance, on one day when her mother read the book to her three times after lunch, Alice (now 8 months) laughed at each page and with each page pointed to and then placed a finger on Spot. Perhaps it was the fact that Spot was engaged in various activities and was in a different position on each page that delighted Alice. Whatever her reasons Alice was always excited by sharing this book.

Spot became a favourite character for Alice and she became interested in other books about him. Among the little Spot board books that she enjoyed was *Spot looks at colours* (Hill, 1986). Each time the book was brought out she would smile at it and gurgle, and increasingly want to hold it for herself and open the pages – although not necessarily starting at the front or looking at each page in order.

Other books, too, appealed to her. Some were picture books with a single object on each page, with its, label – such as *My Toys* (Tucker, 1980), which Alice shared with her father:

F   Now on this page.
     What's this one?
     It's a pedal car isn't it?
     And next to it?

Picture 2: Alice enjoys her book with mother. 7 months.

Picture 3: Looking at the pictures in a book with father. 8 months.

A puppet.
He's got a red hat hasn't he?
(8 months)

As might be expected, there was a sequence to the way each page was brought to Alice's attention: first asking what the object was and then, because Alice could not yet give the answer, labelling it for her. Alice could hold this strong board book herself, look at some of the pages and, occasionally, bite it – teething was still a significant matter.

Then, for a while, *Spot's toy box* (Hill, 1991) became Alice's preferred book. No matter how many times her parents or grandparents shared this book with her she seemed to want to go through it again. Some pages became especial favourites of hers.

F   *Spot's train goes round and round.*
      There it goes round and round.
      Ch-la-loo.
      (9 months)

After the reader pointed the way for the train to go round the track a few times Alice used her finger to point to the track and follow it round a little way. On another page, she pointed to the duck by the side of the bath where Spot was being bathed. Alice may have been making a connection to her own plastic duck and the ducks she watched being fed at the lake.

As well as pointing to objects on the page Alice was using her index finger to encourage the adult to turn the page when she was ready. She began trying to turn the page herself. Alice was manipulating objects and books with greater dexterity every day. Little board books are helpful to very young children because they fit into even the smallest of hands. Alice often picked up *Spot's toy box* from among the toys on the floor, as she crawled around the room, and held it and turned over pages on her own – although not always from front to back – demonstrating some awareness of how to hold a book and how to use it.

Another board book which interested Alice was *Hickory Dickory Dock* (Kemp, 1990). Like most young children, she was prepared to have an adult read it to her countless times a day. She supported these readings by using her index finger to turn the page. Board books have the advantage of helping babies to turn their pages because they can press a finger against the side of a page and so move the page over – which cannot be done with paper. Typically the adult reading the story with Alice would offer a number of comments about the book as each page was turned.

Gf   *Hickory, dickory, dock.*
      The mouse ran up the clock.
      There he is, there's the mouse.
      and you can see the clock can't you?
      The clock struck one,

Bong.
It's one o'clock isn't it?
You can see the time on the clock.
The mouse ran down.
He's coming down fast isn't he?
And he's dropped his bucket.
Hickory, dickory dock.
Look the mouse is on the floor among all the toys.
What toys can you see there?
(10 months)

Alice could not yet answer, but she did look at each picture, and she would point to the train or the mouse when asked where they were. At the end of the reading, she would indicate by trying to turn the pages that what she really wanted was to hear and see the story again. So another reading would follow. With rhyme books like *Hickory Dockory Dock*, the adults tended not to read the words of the book but rather to name objects and describe the actions portrayed in the pictures, as they did with *Animal Friends* (Matthes and Watson, 1986).

Gm   Look there's two ducks on this page.
They're just like the yellow ducks that you play with.
I wonder what they are going to play.
(The text reads – *'What shall we play today?' ask the ducks.*)
(11 months)

But control did not rest solely with the adult: Alice would use the index finger of her right hand to turn the board pages of the book when she wanted to look at the next page.

Naturally, Alice engaged in many different activities over short periods of time. When visiting her grandparents she would crawl around the house, stop to play with the plastic ducks, push and pull on her toy fire engine, take great pleasure in her explorations with empty boxes and paper bags, grasp at ornaments (if not put out of reach), swing doors to and fro, look at own her reflection in windows and mirrors, climb the stairs, pull herself onto her feet by holding on to the sofa or chairs etc.

But she would also crawl to the bookshelf and collect a book from the section where her books were stored. Usually she would place a book on the floor before her and turn the pages over to look at the pictures. Denny Taylor (1983) identified how there is a momentary engagement with print before the baby moves on to other interesting objects and activities. We saw Alice at 11 months often engage thus, at her grandparents' house, with *Baby's Colors* (Ricken, 1990). The small hardboard pages made it an easy book for Alice to manipulate and she appeared to find the bright pictures attractive. Her favourite was the brown page with the picture of teddy bears on it and Alice kept going back to this page and would occasionally kiss one of the teddy bears just as she would her toy teddy.

Although for most of the day Alice would determine which of the many objects or activities she would crawl to, she could also be encouraged to engage with a particular object. Questions such as 'where is the duck?' would set Alice crawling to find it. If asked to 'get a book Alice', she would crawl to the bookshelf to collect one of her books. Alice was not yet talking (at least not in easily distinguishable words) but there were many words that she understood and responded to as she approached her first birthday.

Alice at 1 year old

Obviously, because Alice lived in an environment full of books and had the opportunity to share those books with interested adults we could expect her to demonstrate learning about books and reading. Nevertheless, the amount of learning that had taken place in this first year still seemed surprising – although no doubt typical of many children given similar provision and support.

Physically Alice could handle a book by:
> picking it up or extracting one from a bookshelf,
> orienting the book correctly so it was the right way up,
> turning a page when she wanted to look at the next picture,
> turn the pages from the front towards the back.

Picture 4: Looking at a book on her own. 11 months.

Alice learnt about the language of reading:
> she understood the word 'book',
> 'page', 'picture', 'next', 'start', 'end' were among the words
> she heard frequently and was presumably learning.

She was aware that:
> pictures in a book could represent objects,
> she made connections between pictures, objects in real life

and the name of these objects.

But most important of all she found books:
> interesting to look at and
> she enjoyed sharing a book with an adult.

And Alice's parents and grandparents enjoyed reading with Alice.

Chapter 3
From 1 to 2 years

By the time Alice reached her first birthday she was increasingly making connections between objects or toys in her environment and the pictures in some of her books. Accordingly the adults would draw Alice's attention to a specific picture and relate it to an object nearby.

F There's the ducks.
   Where's the duck Alice?
   Alice show me where the duck is.

Alice would respond by pointing at a duck (or to be more precise stabbing the duck with her index finger). Occasionally she would kiss the duck instead. The adult began to link the book to a nearby object.

   Where's your duck Alice?
   Alice get the duck.

And off Alice would crawl or walk (as she was by now taking a few steps) to get her plastic duck.

   That's just like the duck in the picture isn't it?
   There's Alice's duck.
   And there's the duck in the picture.
   (1 year)

The animated Kipling characters in the Disney version of *Jungle Book* (Disney, 1993) elicited similar connections. Alice enjoyed playing with her plastic toys Baloo, ShereKhan and King Louis and then pointing to the characters in the Disney version of the book. Her involvement was extended further because she liked watching short extracts of her Disney Jungle Book video.

Adults predictably raise their own expectations of what children can do, in this context contributing to the sharing of a book. Adults used intonation and pauses to encourage Alice to take an active role in sharing a book. For instance on an occasion when she was yet again sharing *Animal Friends* (Matthes and Watson, 1986), she responded to her grandmother's comments and questions:

Gm   What's here then?
            Is that the ducks?
A   duh duh
Gm   That's right it's the ducks.
            And there's the cat.
            Stroke the cat.
A   (Alice strokes the cat).
Gm   Oh, what does the pig do?
A   ugh ugh
Gm   Who's this?
            Is it the dog?
A   duh duh
       (1 year 1 month)

Such encounters with books were brief but frequent. Most usually they provided interludes between walking – and falling over, opening cupboards – and emptying them if given enough time, building with bricks – but knocking them down when they reached two or at most a three levels high, cuddling soft toys and climbing the stairs. Sharing a book seemed to offer a short respite before Alice embarked on further explorations.

Alice displayed her language competence and memory when responding to the various comments, questions and requests made by the adults around her. So when asked to:

> Bring your Jungle Book Alice,

she was able to toddle to a bookcase in her home, pick up the first book in her pile of books and discard it, do the same with the second book and take the third book and bring this one, *Jungle Book* (Disney,

1993), to the adult. She demonstrated her understanding of the words used, her memory of the title and the book, and a recognition that this was the one required from her collection of books. She also expected that an adult would share the book with her, so when she brought it to the adult she promptly sat on the floor in front of the adult, waiting to have the book shared, even if only very briefly, before she went off to explore other parts of the room.

During the early months of Alice's second year an insistent feature of each day was her questions about the objects in her environment. Initially the questions took one of two forms: 'Whatisit' or 'Whoisit', each sounding more like a single word than a sentence. Her other main utterance at this time was 'Isit', when she appeared to be satisfied by the responses that she received from the adults. These questions, and acceptance of an answer, were applied to the sharing of books. So when sharing *Jungle Book*, Alice would ask:

A   Whatisit?
Gm   That's the elephants, isn't it?
A   Whatisit?
Gm   It's the elephants.
       They're big aren't they?
A   Whatisit?
Gm   The elephants.
A   Isit?
Gm   Mmh.
       That's the elephants.
       They're on parade aren't they?
       (1 year 2 months)

The adults who shared books with Alice had to be prepared to name the main objects pictured in them and often to repeat this over and over until Alice's curiosity about each picture was satisfied. And Alice might well turn back to the front page when the book was finished and ask her questions again to get the adult to restart the process of naming the objects in each picture.

Picture 5: Alice talks about her book. 1 year 2 months.

At her grandparents' house Alice had a small book collection kept on a low shelf of a bookcase in the dining room. During her visits she spent time looking through them as she wandered around the house. She could also select a book and take it to an adult to share.

Gf   Alice get your Panda book.
        Get your Panda book from the other room.
A   (Alice leaves the room and returns with the Panda book)
Gf   Good girl.
        Have you got the Panda book?
        Come on then let's have a look at it.
        There's Panda.
        And who's he with?
A   Whoisit?
Gf   That's the penguin isn't it?
        The penguin's black and white, just like Panda.
        (1 year 3 months)

This continued with her grandfather naming the various animals and their attributes. Alice made a number of contributions to the sharing, pointing to animals but mostly asking questions.

Although Alice did not say many words clearly yet she did demonstrate an understanding of words and communications. When asked to get the Panda book – *Panda's Friends at the Zoo* (Teeney Books, 1991) outside of her own home, she still showed that she understood by going to get the book, also that she could memorise the task by getting the book from one room and bringing it back to another. She could discriminate between the books on the shelves and select the correct book, and she was obviously motivated, collecting the book and bringing it to share with an adult. She also enjoyed joining in with language games:

      Ring a ring of roses.
      A pocket full of poses.
      Atishoo, atishoo
      we all fall down.

> Fishes in the water,
> fishes in the sea.
> We all jump up,
> with a one, two, three.

She would fall down and jump up in unison with this rhyme. Then there were her telephone 'conversations'. She had observed adults making telephone conversations and occasionally had the telephone placed against her ear when someone in the family called. At fifteen months she would pause as she passed the telephone, pick it up, place it correctly against her ear and then converse:

A   Hao (the 'll' was not part of her Hello)
       Ba-ba-ba-ba
       (1 year 3 months)

Then she would be replace the telephone, although seldom correctly. Her consistent use of 'Hao', with appropriate intonation, suggested an awareness of some of the conventions of telephone conversations.

Alice remained interested in the various animals that she saw in real life, on the television or in books. In particular her interest in ducks was rekindled by a visit to a lake where she fed the birds with bread and was soon surrounded by ducks. A few days later a new book, *Duck's Friends on the Pond* (Teeney Books, 1991) was placed in among her collection of books at her grandparents' home. Shortly after she arrived for a visit she was asked to get her duck book – as yet unseen:

Gf   Alice shall we look at the Duck book?
       See if you can find the duck book.
A   (Alice goes to her book collection and picks books from the
       pile until she reaches the duck book, which she brings to the
       adult).
Gf   That's it.
       It's a Duck book.
       Who's that?
A   Duck

Picture 6: Sharing a book with grandfather. 1 year 2 months.

Gf   It is isn't it?
        On this page he's saying
            Hello Fish, where are you going?

A   Duck
        Yes, that's the duck.
        (1 year 4 months)

Thus Alice was able to make the connection from an experience and an image of duck, via the word to her new book. Subsequently her contribution to the discussion and reading of the book was to say 'duck' – with a heavy emphasis upon the /d/ and /ck/ – as each page was turned. And, as we might expect from very young children, she made frequent requests for the book to be read again.

Although there were many objects to be explored in the house and outside in the garden, Alice regularly stopped to look at her books more than once each day, whether she was at home or at her grandparents'. During those engagements with her books three features of her behaviour were notable: intensity, concentration and control. The intensity of her involvement was most easily observed when she engaged with an oversize book, and one could watch her attention moving from one object to another, staring at some image for a moment and then moving her eyes to look at another. She would sit on the floor with a book in front of her and go through it from front to back. She would then repeat the whole process or select another book to look through. Such spells of concentration, on her own, could last for twenty minutes before she would get up and wander off to do something else. She had control of her time with the books but she also exerted control over the adults who shared a book with her:

A	(Alice, sitting on the floor, has the book *Animal Friends* (Matthes and Watson, 1986) in front of her). What'sthat?
Gf	That's the hedgehog.
A	What'sthat?
Gf	That's the baby hedgehog, isn't it?
A	(Alice turns to the next page) What'sthat? (pointing to a badger).
Gf	That's a badger, can you see his black and white face.
A	(Alice points to another badger on the page.)
Gf	That's another badger.
A	(Alice points to the third badger.)
Gf	That's a badger as well.
A	(Points to the first badger.)
Gf	Badger.
A	(Points to the next badger.)
Gf	Badger.
A	(Alice, laughing, points to each badger in turn.)
Gf	Badger, badger, badger... (1 year 5 months)

On this occasion Alice appeared to get immense pleasure from controlling the response of the adults, particularly by speeding up her pointing at each badger and so accelerating their response. Alice was very much in control.

Young children appear to delight in the rhythm and rhyme of finger games, nursery rhymes and activities guided by language (Opie and Opie, 1959). Alice was no exception and she demonstrated her enjoyment of rhymes when sharing *Here's a Happy Pig* (Hawkins and Hawkins, 1987). This board book has finger holes cut into it so the adult, and eventually the child as she becomes more dextrous, can wiggle a finger in the finger holes of each picture to create ears, tails and tongue:

Gf   *Here's a yappy dog*
                wagging his tail.
A   (Alice grabs hold of wagging tail)....

On the back cover is a short rhyme placed above the four finger holes for the previous page. This rhyme amused Alice and had to be repeated frequently:

Gf   *One! Two! Three!*
                Wiggle and see!
A   (Alice laughs).
Gf   Shall I read that again?
A   Ta.

Gf   *One! Two! Three!*
                Wiggle and see!
A   (Alice laughs).
        Ta
Gf   *One! Two! Three!*
                Wiggle and see! ...
        (1 year 6 months)

We cannot be certain just what amused Alice but she did appear to like the way the two lines rhymed. If so, that interest and enjoyment might ultimately be to Alice's advantage as a reader. An awareness of rhyme in the early years has been linked to later progress in reading (Goswami and Bryant, 1990). Alice was hearing and enjoying those rhymes regularly, in the familiar setting of shared book reading.

Word for word reading of a book was still rare. Usually the pictures were discussed, particulary the objects or characters in the illustrations. Or the adult might tell a story derived from the pictures, especially when a book seemed more wordy than would suit her just yet. For instance, Alice enjoyed sharing a *Bambi* (Disney, 1990) book – which she could relate to images of a video that she watched from time to time, but she seemed more interested in the pictures and hearing an adult develop a story linked to them (as well as being guided by the text):

Gf	*One day, as the sun rose, there was*
	great excitement in the forest.
	Because there was a new baby in the forest called Bambi.
	And all the animals and birds came to see him.
	There's Thumper.
	What does he do?
A	puh puh puh
Gf	Yes, and there's the bluebirds.
	Now.
	First Bambi couldn't stand but,
	Then he got to his feet...
	(1 year 7 months)

And so the story-telling continued with, on this occasion, some words read from the book and some comments about the pictures, the text and the pictures serving as a guide. Carol Fox (1993) among others who have looked at young children growing up with stories, observes that story tellings, as well as story readings, are an important feature of the children's early experiences.

Like many young children, Alice had several colourful posters in her bedroom. One was a large alphabet wall frieze (Early Learning Centre, n.d.), which her parents used on most days when Alice climbed onto her bed so that she was on a level with the frieze. Typically her mother or father would talk about the pictures, name the objects and state the letter of the alphabet. Eventually this turned into a game, which Alice loved and wanted repeated over and over. The parent would just name the letter and Alice would respond, generally with physical actions or a form of sign language, rather than naming the objects:

F	<T> is for?
A	aah. (Cuddles an imaginary teddy bear)
F	<U> is for?
A	(Holds out hand to check for rain – umbrella)
F	And the <V> is for?
A	brm brm (van)
F	<W> is for the?
A	(Holds up her hand and looks at her wrist – the object in the picture being a wristwatch) ...
	(1 year 8 months)

As we might expect from children of this age, Alice used the sound of the object in some cases ('brm brm' for van) while naming others e.g. 'hus' for house and physically demonstrating many others e.g. holding out her hand to check for rain, for umbrella. These interactions indicate that Alice could recognise the spoken letter names and associate these with the object which appeared alongside the letter on her frieze. The fact that she was able to respond to the letter names when they were given out of sequence and away from her bedroom would indicate that she was indeed recognising the letter names spoken by her parents and could make those connections.

When adults are reading with very young children the naming of objects is a common feature. We saw how in some early interactions the adult would ask Alice 'Where is the duck?' or 'Who is that?' Ninio and Bruner (1978) suggested that typically adults use language:

- to gain the attention of the child

- to ask what the object is

- to provide a label when the child needs one

- to let the child know whether he/she was right (give feedback).

All this applied when adults read to Alice. However, Alice could take on a similar role for herself, at least in part.

On one occasion Alice collected her *Forest Friends* book (Matthes and Watson, 1986b) and brought it to me to share. On the cover is a picture of a deer and a field mouse.

A   (Alice holds the book in front of herself)
        (points to the deer)
        deer
Gf   It is isn't it, that's the deer.
A   What's that?
Gf   That's the mouse.
A   (Alice turns the page)
        Who's that?
Gf   You know who that is.
A   Who's it?
GF   It's the fox.
A   Who's that? (points to the owls on the opposite page)
Gf   You know who that is too.
        Who is it?
A   owl (spoken with an extended sounding of the l)
Gf   It is isn't it .
        It's the owl....
        (1 year 9 months)

So right from the start, Alice used some of the strategies normally adopted the adult. She had pointed to one of the animals – was that to gain my attention? She had labelled one of the animals. And she had asked about an animal even though she could name it herself – 'who's that?' and 'owl'. In part, perhaps, Alice had learned a routine during these book sharings. But she may also have been using the questioning in that way because it would give her the answers that she needed at that point in her language development. What hadn't changed was the almost inevitable urging to begin again once the last page was reached. The occasions when one single reading of a book would suffice remained rare.

Alice's oral vocabulary grew rapidly at this time and she appeared to want to use her new vocabulary when looking at a book. Indeed, she gave emphasis to naming the objects she knew and this would encourage the adult to confirm or reject that naming. For instance the last two pages of *Jungle Friends* (Spurgeon, 1994) demonstrated her frequent naming. The double page has a picture of four elephants beside a pool of water. There are six lines of verse on the page, although that was ignored by both Alice and the adult during this sharing.

A	daddy
Gf	It is the daddy elephant, isn't it?
A	mummy
Gf	Yes, that's the mummy elephant.
A	baby
Gf	That's the baby elephant.
A	ear
Gf	He's got big ears, hasn't he?
A	eye
Gf	And tiny eyes.
A	sea
Gf	Mmh, it is like the sea. It might be a river or a lake.
	(1 year 10 months)

For the moment Alice had run out of names for the objects in the picture so she returned to the beginning and again looked at each double page and named what she could. Mainly this was to rehearse the six words she had used on the elephant page although on some pages she added the word 'nose' – though never in connection with the elephant's trunk.

Although her use of 'baby', 'mummy' and 'daddy' seemed to be linked appropriately to the animal pictures in this book she was probably not being so accurate. In other circumstances she could be seen to use those words to mean small, bigger and biggest. For instance, when she played with her wooden building bricks and placed chimneys (circular blocks) on top of any structure, she would refer to the three sizes of blocks as 'baby imney', 'mummy imney' and 'daddy imney'. But as well as using these words to relate to size, she used them more conventionally – such as when sharing the book.

'Oh dear' was another phrase that Alice now used for a number of purposes. When she did something of which she knew her parents would disapprove; if she couldn't manage a task; when she knocked over her building bricks; if a cloud covered the moon!... any and all of these might evoke the comment 'Oh dear'. Friends of Alice's parents took note and bought her the book *Oh Dear!* (Rod Campbell, 1983) for Christmas and Alice quickly took to the story and contributed to its telling. The story is about Buster, who visits his Grandma on the farm and helps her by going to fetch some eggs, visiting several wrong places before reaching the hen house:

Gf	*So he went to the hutch*
	and asked the ...
	Who's that?
A	puh puh
Gf	Yes, the rabbit goes puh puh
	No eggs here!
A	*Oh dear!*
Gf	*Oh dear!*
	So he went to the pond
	and asked the ...
A	*duck*
Gf	*the duck.*
	No eggs here!
A	*Oh dear!*

(1 year 11 months)

Each of Buster's visits concludes with the lines: 'No eggs here! Oh dear!'. This infuses rhythm and repetition that children seem to enjoy and which encourages their participation. Alice liked to complete each page by pronouncing a very emphatic 'Oh dear!' each time the story was read to her. Although Alice was not reading in the conventional sense of looking at the print and identifying each word, she was taking part in the reading by remembering the last line and inserting it appropriately. She knew not to say 'Oh dear' at the end of the first or last page, where the phrase does not appear.

Although Alice had taken part in story readings by naming animals or responding to questions, her speaking a line from the book on each of the seven pages where it occurred, seemed to be a big step forward. Her comment 'Oh dear!' linked in perfectly with the text, so made her an active contributor to the story reading. As she approached her second birthday, Alice's literacy development appeared to have moved forward significantly. Furthermore, she had also become interested in 'writing'. Her father would frequently write at home and inevitably Alice became interested and wanted to write when he did.

A	pen
F	Ask mummy for your pen and writing book.
A	(Goes to her mother)
	pen
M	Do you want your pen and your book?
A	ta
M	Here you are.
	Sit here if you want to write.
A	(Alice makes circular movements with the pen on the paper)
	(1 year 11 months)

Thus Alice was beginning to adopt a new role during story readings and to develop an interest in writing. However, her world was changing in other significant ways too. Just before her second birthday the arrival of her sister, Caitlin, created other interests for Alice.

Alice at 2 years old

As she reached her second birthday Alice continued to be supported in her literacy development she retained her interest in books – which she demonstrated by:

collecting a book to look at by herself,
collecting a book to take to an adult to share,
(the involvement with a book would occur at any time of
day   as Alice moved from one play activity to another).

Furthermore when encouraged by an adult, Alice was able to:
select a specific book, from a collection of books,
point to objects or characters in the illustrations,
name many of the objects or characters in the illustrations,
make connections to real life from the objects/characters in
a book.

Alice demonstrated that she was able to use a book competently by:
orienting the book so front and top were placed correctly,
turning the pages from front to back,
finding a specific page.

During the shared story readings Alice would take control from time to time or join in the reading by:
pointing to an object or character,
asking about them e.g. 'Who is it?'
naming, objects or characters, without being asked,
reading lines of text which provided the rhythm and
repetition to help her memorise the phrase.

In addition to the shared story readings Alice had experience of:
an alphabet frieze and games involving the recognition of
the   spoken names of letters,
various rhymes including popular nursery rhymes,
writing – albeit just making circular movements with her pen
on paper.

These other experiences of literacy – shared with an adult as an enjoyable activity – would also contribute to Alice's literacy development.

Chapter 4
From 2 to 3 years

On Alice's second birthday a number of birthday cards arrived, most addressed to 'Alice'. Some had her forename and family name, and the ones delivered by hand had no address. So her name stood out quite boldly on most of the envelopes:

F   Here's another birthday card for you Alice.

A   Ta.

F   There you are.
It says Alice (pointing to the forename)

A   <p> (pointing to the <p> in her surname)

F   Yes, it is the letter <p>, isn't it.
(2 years)

Her recognition of a letter and the naming of it came as something of a surprise. However, a link might be made to Alice's alphabet frieze and the game she often played with her parents, which went something like this:

M   <P> is for?

A   parrot

M   It is the parrot isn't it.

Presumably Alice had learnt not only about the object associated with the letter but also to recognise and name certain letters. And on her second birthday she did that away from the usual context of the alphabet frieze and recognised the letter <p> among the other letters on the envelope.

Alice was also continuing to make small contributions to shared readings. She continued to do so with *Oh Dear!* and she also began to chime in with familar rhymes. There are numerous collections of well known nursery rhymes with bold illustrations. One such, *Nursery Rhymes – 1* (Holland Enterprises, n.d.), is a hardboard book with three rhymes. Alice enjoyed the rhyme 'Polly put the kettle on':

Gf	Shall we read about Polly again?
A	ta
Gf	*Polly put the kettle on,*
	Polly put the kettle on,
	Polly put the kettle on,
	We'll all have some
A	*tea.*
	(2 years)

I probably read to a young child no differently than other adults do. Knowing that Alice was familiar with the rhyme my rising intonation towards the end of each verse invited her to provide the last word in the verse. Alice enjoyed doing this and indeed appeared to anticipate it, watching me saying the lines aloud rather than looking at the book as we shared the rhyme.

There was a further insight into Alice's growing recognition of letter shapes when she sat at the piano to use the keyboard (although I refrain from calling it playing the piano). When she paused in this musical activity she suddenly pointed to one of the letters in the name of the makers of the piano – CHAPPELL – printed in upper case letters.

A	<P>
Gm	It is the letter <P>, isn't it.
	and there are some other letters aren't there?
A	<C>
Gm	That is a <C>.
A	<H>

Gm	\<H\>
A	\<A\>
Gm	Yes, an \<A\>.
A	\<E\>
Gm	It is an \<E\>.
	(2 years 1 month)

Although Alice had reached the letter L and appeared to look at it, she made no comment about it and went back to exploring the notes of the piano. Nevertheless, that brief episode with print indicated that Alice had learned to recognise some letters, and that this learning was incidental and presumably largely derived from the games played with her parents with her alphabet frieze.

Alice also continued to enjoy sharing books. And after a fall of snow, which Alice played with for a few days, *The Snowman* (Briggs, 1994) became one of her favourite choices. The hardboard version has the added attraction of various 'Things to Touch and Feel, See and Sniff'. Alice particularly liked to touch the Snowman's green woolly scarf, to look at her reflection in the Christmas tree ornament and to smell 'Mum's perfume'. She also liked to make comments about each of the pictures:

A	Snowman
Gf	That's the Snowman again.
A	Balloons
Gf	Yes, there are lots of balloons, aren't there?
A	Up high.
Gf	That one is up high.
A	Green one.
Gf	It's green.
A	A baby green one.
Gf	It is small, isn't it.
A	Blue
Gf	Blue
A	Purple

Gf   It is a purple one isn't it?
       (2 years 1 month)

Alice's oral vocabulary was growing rapidly and this was reflected in the contribution that she made whenever a book was shared. Her comments were now increasingly of more than one word: 'Up high', 'Green one' and 'A baby green one' exemplify the development in her speech.

Alice's naming of letters and her contributions to shared readings continued to develop. One Sunday she picked up a discarded Weekend Magazine from one of the national newspapers, placed it in front of herself on the floor and announced:

A   Reading.
M   You're reading are you?
A   A'ice reading.   (The 'l' sound did not yet appear in Alice's
                            pronunciation of her name).
M   Yes.
        And what letters can you see in that word? (*Weekend*)
A   <e>
M   Mmh.
        How many <e>'s are there?
A   One, two, three. (Three was the current extent of her
                           counting).
M   There are three, aren't there?
A   <p>
M   It is like a <p> isn't it?
        That one is a <d> though.
A   <d>
M   Yes, it's a <d>.
        (2 years 1 month)

Not surprisingly, certain lower case letters caused her some confusion, for instance between<d> and <p>. These letters, like <b> and <q>, are composed of a vertical line joined to a half-circle. The importance of the orientation of the letter would require more experience with print.

Picture 7: Reading the Weekend Magazine. 2 years 1 month.

Alice's print experience was coming from a number of sources but most especially from the frequent shared story readings. Now on the very first reading of a new book, *The Bus Stop* (Hellen, 1988), Alice contributed to the reading. Her contribution was naturally aided by the nature of this story, which repeats the same question on every page until the story is resolved on the final page. From the first page, the writing brings the listener into the story:

Gf   Shall we look at this new book?

A   Ta.

Gf   You can see the Bus Stop by the side of the road. (Looking at the cover).

A   Daisies.

Gf   Yes, there are some daisies by the road.

A   Sun.

Gf   And the sun is shining.

     And what's this where the road goes over the river?

A   Bridge.

Gf   It's a bridge.

     But there's nothing on the road.

     Let's find out shall we?

         This is the bus stop

         outside Littleton village...

         ...but can you see the bus yet?

A   No.

It is the question '*...but can you see the road yet?* which is repeated on the next six pages as people form the queue for the bus and which encourages the child to become involved in the story. Alice enjoyed answering the question.

In subsequent readings of the book – and it had to be repeated many times on the first day she shared it – Alice contributed more to the story, including some of the key words:

Gf   *Second is*

A   *Jane*

Gf	*Jackson starting off*
	on her way to
A	*School.*
Gf	*...but can you see the bus yet?*
A	No.

(2 years 1 month)

Alice's contribution of '*Jane*' and '*school*' were derived from her memory of the story, the characters in it, and their destination. She was not reading the print nor problably even looking at it. Instead she appeared to be engrossed in closely examining each character as he/she joined the queue at the bus stop. Nevertheless, the nature of the book and, on reflection, my intonation as I read to Alice encouraged her to take part in the reading and to contribute more with, it seemed, each reading.

At this time Alice also acted as the reader (or adult), showing a book to her two month old sister Caitlin. It was unlikely that Caitlin was able to profit by such showings as Alice usually held the book an inch or so from her face where she could not possibly focus on the pictures. But it was interesting to note this role-play with books, among the many role-play activities in which Alice now engaged.

A few weeks later Alice's response to *The Bus Stop* had altered significantly. In particular she now commented about each of the characters in the story and their destination and she no longer answered the question – 'but can you see the bus yet?':

Gf	*This is the bus stop outside Littleton village*
	but
A	*but*
Gf	*can you see the*
A	*bus yet?*
Gf	There's no bus there yet.
	First comes Mrs
A	*Bishop.*

Gf	*She's going*
A	*shopping*
Gf	*in town.*
	(2 years 2 months)

Although Alice was no longer responding with the repeated question in the book she contributed to the reading of the question. So on each page she would echo the adult reading 'but' and then provide the last two words of the question: 'bus yet?' And perhaps because she was now partly asking the question she saw no reason to provide the answer, as she had done a few weeks earlier. The account of a reading above also shows how she would typically give some part of the name of the person in the picture and say where they were off to or what they were going to do, indicating Alice's involvement with the story and how she memorised so much of it.

Some picture books written for young children are designed to en-courage interactions between the reader and the listener. *Who Says Moo?* (Young, 1994) is one such text. Each double spread contains a picture of an animal, or animals, with a question about it or them. The questions invite a response from the listener. Take as an example two of the double-spreads mid-way through the book:

Gf	*Who looks up?*
A	Hedgehog.
Gf	*Who looks down?*
A	Giraffe.
Gf	It is the giraffe with its long neck.
	Who is pink?
A	Pig.
	In a field.
Gf	Yes, it's in a field.
	Who is brown?
A	It's a bear.
Gf	Yes, it's a bear.
A	And a bee.
Gf	Yes, there is a bee in that picture.
	(2 years 3 months)

Picture 8: Another reading of Who Says Moo. *2 years 2 months.*

Alice was probably not exceptional in responding so positively to the question and answer sequence. She enjoyed looking at the pictures, hearing the question, providing an answer and adding comments about other features she noticed e.g. 'In a field' and 'And a bee'. The adult has to ensure that there is no test-like pressure on the child during such an interaction, but where the enjoyment of the book is the prime purpose and the adult supplies answers whenever required, this is unlikely.

Alice's interest in animals was also reflected in her television watching. She enjoyed a number of nature programmes – although she was inclined to wander off if a narrator appeared on the screen for any length of time. While watching a programme on giraffes she indicated an awareness of print (or of TV programme conventions). Perhaps because the programme concentrated on the giraffes (although elephants, zebras and lions also put in brief appearances) she watched the programme right through for the full twenty-five minutes, and when the first of the closing captions appeared on the screen, she immediately waved and said 'Bye-bye giraffes'.

There were other indications that Alice was discriminating between pictures and writing. Her own drawings and writing could now be separated. For instance a drawing of some named person would be based on a large circle and in it two eyes, a nose and a mouth. On occasions she might put some hair on top of the head. But when she wrote, horizontal lines were her most common representation.

While sharing a favourite book of hers (*Jungle Friends*; Spurgeon, 1994), she demonstrated her awareness of print when she reached the elephant's page towards the end of the book:

A   Elephant, trunk.
Gf   He's getting the water with his trunk.
A   Shower.
Gf   Yes, he's having a shower.
A   Elephants.
       Alice reading.
Gf   You are reading the book.
       Where's the writing?
A   (Puts her finger on the block of writing).
       (2 years 4 months)

Perhaps at this time she saw those six lines of writing as six horizontal lines rather than as letters and words conveying a meaning. Nevertheless, she was able to locate the writing on the double page in front of her.

On other occasions Alice took an active part in story reading, especially with the short books she had shared often at home with her parents. Alice was observed reading one of these books, *Tuffy the Jeep* (Pillinger, n.d.) with her mother. In this instance, the story line, rhythm and rhyme were the sole features of the shared reading:

Picture 9: Alice writing and drawing. 2 years 2 months.

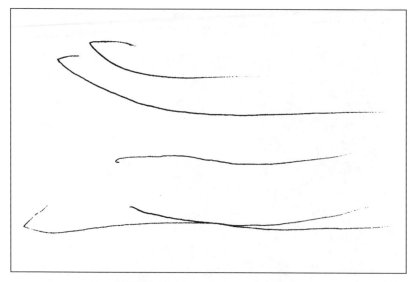

Figure 1: Alice's writing. 2 years 3 months.

(The words in brackets indicate words that Alice omitted).

M	*Down through*
	the river
A	*(and) up the bank.*
M	*He's*
A	*so strong.*
	(He's) like (a) tank.
M	*Over sharp rocks.*
A	*Out (of) tight squeezes.*
M	*Tuffy can go.*
A	*Wherever he pleases.*
	(2 years 4 months)

The few words that Alice omitted were mainly, articles (the, a), prepositions (to, of) and conjunctions (and) and these omissions did not distract from the story rhyme. It may well have been the rhyme which enabled Alice to take such an active part in the story because she was lying on the floor recalling parts of the story but not looking at the words, while her mother sat in a chair and read from the book.

Alice demonstrated a great deal of enthusiasm for any new book she was offered. Her enjoyment was evident and she would make comments and ask questions about it and ask for it to be read over and over again. For instance, *Baby Owl* (O'Neill, 1990) was introduced to her one evening before she went off to bed:

A	It's a new book.
Gf	It is isn't it?
A	Yes.
Gf	What is it about, do you think? (Looking at the cover)
A	A bird.
Gf	It is a bird.
	What kind of bird is it?
A	A brown bird.
Gf	Yes, it is brown.
	It's an owl.
A	Yes, owl.
Gf	And who is this?
A	It's a baby one.
Gf	Baby owl.
A	Baby owl.

This initial discussion was followed by a complete reading of the book to Alice to which, quite unusually, Alice listened in full without making a comment. However, she soon made up for that silence:

A	Read it again.
Gf	*Baby owl lives in a tree with her mother.*
A	Baby owl.
Gf	Yes, that's the baby owl.
A	With her mummy.
Gf	Yes, that's baby owl with her mother.
A	Ladybird.
Gf	There's a ladybird on the tree isn't there?
A	Yes.
Gf	Now.

A	'nother ladybird.

Gf	Yes, and

Baby owl's brothers and sisters live there, too.

A	Looking.

Gf	They are looking out from the nest, aren't they?

When this second reading was completed Alice again repeated her request: 'Read it again'.

She appeared to want to look at each picture and talk about what she could see in it, rather than concentrating on the words of the story, although she did hear the words on each repeat reading. After the first few readings she joined in with the reading at a few points and especially the ending:

Gf	*...her mother flies home, and the owls sleep*
A	*all day long!*

Her recognition of the ending was probably aided by her enjoyment and knowledge of a nursery song with the same last line –

> (*The wheels on the bus go round and round,*
> *all day long.*)

Once Alice was satisfied with the repeated readings she wanted to show the book to other people:

A	It's the owl book.
M	It is the owl.
A	There's the flowers.
M	They are lovely flowers aren't they?
A	The owl is flying to find food.
M	And who's going to get the food?
A	Baby owl.

As this book was introduced to Alice so late close to bedtime, she had to take the book to bed with her and when she was fast asleep, the book had to be gently prised from her hands and placed beside her bed. The following morning Alice came out of her bedroom holding the book and announcing to anyone who wished to listen:

A   Baby owl.

(2 years 5 months)

So the process of sharing the book with Alice had to begin again and just as on the previous evening, it required a number of readings before Alice left the book to wander off to other attractions.

As Alice reached the age of two and half she continued to share books with the key adults in her life but her involvement with literacy extended in other ways that revealed her emerging literacy. I noted eight occasions when Alice (2 years 6 months) gave an indication of her literacy understanding and knowledge – and there must have been many other examples which I missed.

1) Alice asked if she could 'do drawing'. That meant that she wanted to be supplied with paper and crayons and to sit at the table to draw.

The first picture was announced to be 'grandad', and she drew the 'smiling' mouth below the two eyes and the nose in a large circle. Alongside this picture were written seven squiggles, or pseudoletters. As she wrote them, she named them: <d>, <d>, <b>, <i>, <d>.

Next she drew 'grandma' and this also had squiggles alongside the picture, which were announced as <m>, <m>, <e>, <m>. It was interesting to note the substantial use of <d>s with the picture of grandad and <m>s with grandma. A few days later Alice drew a picture of 'shark' (following a visit to a zoo) and added squiggles which were announced to be <c>, <c>, <d>, <c>, <e>.

As Alice wrote on one sheet of paper she indicated that she was 'writing Alice'. This sheet contained three pseudoletters, of which two were like an <l> with a vertical line and the third like a <v> or <u>. This writing showed an interest in representing her own name – which was to develop over the next few months.

2) On a visit to a supermarket Alice helped to put the purchases into the trolley. But when she was told on approaching the next aisle that the next item was 'custard powder', Alice announced: 'Alice get it'. And from the vast array of products in that section she was able to

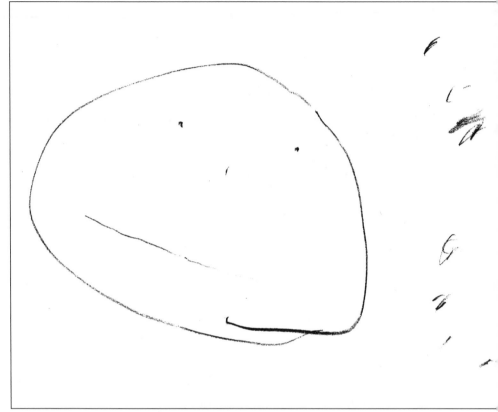

Figure 2: Grandad smiling and d, d, b, i, d. 2 years 5 months.

make the correct choice, presumably by using her memory of shape, colours and logo.

3) During a car journey Alice started to sing, then to hum and to vocalise a rhythm 'ba ba ba' 'ba ba ba'. I repeated this rhythm then suggested 'ba ba, ba ba'. Alice copied that variation so we started on a game with me initiating 'bi bi bi', copied by Alice. Whatever the variation, e.g. 'be be be' and 'bo bo bo', Alice was able to repeat the sounds, which suggests developing phonemic awareness – but the real point was the fun we had with the game.

4) Alice was observed playing by herself with two rag dolls – providing a running commentary as she played. She set the dolls at either end of a sofa, then collected the newspaper from the corner of the room, pulled out a few sheets for each doll and placed them on the dolls' legs in front of them. 'Dolls reading the newspaper' she announced to herself and anyone else in hearing.

5) A quiet house was unusual and typically evoked the question: 'Where's Alice'. On one such occasion she was found sitting at the computer and tapping away at the keyboard while calling out letters <a> <a> <d> <b> <a> etc. Fortunately the computer was off. Alice appeared to recognise that writing could be done with not only pen and paper but also at the computer.

6) Alice began asking: 'Can I have an <o>?' when she wanted a mint from an adult. She had apparently recognised that the 'mint with a hole' was like the letter <o>. She transferred this recognition to all circular mints and for a time they became <o>s.

7) Young children recognise McDonald's from an early age. Studies of other children's experiences with print e.g. Baghban (1984) and Laminack (1991) suggest that in their second or third year they recognise the 'M' logo or the name and associated colour. On a car journey with Alice we passed a McDonald's away from her usual environment:

A   McDonald's
Gf   It is McDonald's
        What do you get there?
A   Chips and a hamburger.
Gf   Mm. Anything else?
A   Pancakes.
Gf   What about to drink?
A   Milkshake.

Later in the journey Alice recognised a truck announcing 'Sainsbury's'. She was recognising and noting the print in her environment – clear evidence of the value of talking to young children about signs and print.

Picture 10: Alice using the computer. 2 years 6 months.

8) Alice was looking at one of her favourite books and as she went back to the beginning and opened the book again at the front she was confronted with one of the title pages which reads:

> *Who*
> *Says*
> *Moo?*

Alice looked at the page and the writing and said:

A   *Who*
               Says
               Moo?

However, as she said each of the three words she ran her finger along the word 'Who'. So, although she recognised the title page as print and understood that there were three words there and that the squiggles were the title words, she could not yet associate each line with a word.

All these examples tell us about Alice's literacy learning and remind us of the wealth of learning that is occurring outside of shared readings. The final example was particularly indicative of the learning taking place in contact with books and especially when an adult is there to support and share the book with her.

A few weeks later, after exploring new books at her usual voracious pace, Alice returned to *Who Says Moo?* (Young, 1994). On opening it at the title page, Alice said promptly:

A   *Who*
          Says
          Moo?
     (2 years 7 months)

This time she pointed to each word as she spoke it. Presumably, her experiences with other shared readings and her observations of the model of reading provided by the adults had enabled her to construct further her understanding of print (Goodman, 1990).

Although Alice demonstrated her increased understanding of print with a book which had been read previously, her attention and interest had moved on. Like many young children, she had become fascinated by dinosaurs – any television programme involving dinosaurs had to be watched, books on dinosaurs had to be borrowed from the library and she pestered her parents constantly to purchase yet another plastic dinosaur. Every time she went off on a family visit her large box of dinosaur models had to come too.

Like other young children, Alice quickly became familiar with the names of different dinosaurs and could readily distinguish them. She demonstrated her knowledge and interest when looking at a non-fiction book, *The Great Dinosaur Atlas* (Lindsay, 1991). She was encouraged to tell her soft toy, Badger, all about the book:

A   Look, I've got Pteranodon, Diplodocus, Stegosaurus, and that one, and Triceratops and that one.
There's my friend, Triceratops. He's got three horns. That's his bones.
Tyrannosaurus Rex with big teeth.
Brachiosaurus, I think, with a long tail. He's got a long neck. He eats leaves.
That's footprints, Badger.
Iguanodon.
Protoceratops, babies in the eggs, Badger.
(2 years 7 months)

The reference here to 'my friend Triceratops' indicated Alice's preference at this time and there were days when Triceratops had to watch Alice eat her dinner!

One television programme with a dinosaur character (or at least a dinosaur type) was Barney. Barney was a large purple dinosaur with human qualities. Because she had seen him on television, Alice immediately recognised the Barney book, *A Day with Barney* (Dudko and Larsen, 1994) and was very excited about the book:

Gf   I've got a new book.
A   It's Barney!
Gf   It is Barney, isn't it.
A   He's stretching.
Gf   Yes. he's just woken up.
      Shall we see what he's doing?
A   Yes.
Gf   *Ring! Ring! Ring!*
            It's time to wake up, Barney!
A   Barney's smiling.
Gf   It does look as though he's smiling, yes.
      (Alice turned the page)
Gf   *Yum! Yum! Yum!*
            What are you eating for breakfast, Barney.

A	Cornflakes.
Gf	Is it cornflakes?
A	Yes.
Gf	Where are they?
A	(Alice pointed to the box of cornflakes)
	And a melon.
Gf	Or, it might be grapefruit.
A	No, it's an orange.
Gf	And?
A	A banana (Alice turned the page).
	There's Baby Bop.
Gf	Yes.

Barney plays with his friend Baby Bop.
(2 years 8 months)

Although there was a discussion about each of the pages, Alice moved the shared reading on quite quickly, turning each page after a few moments. When the book was completed, she requested a repeat reading of it, and then more. With each reading more features were debated and frequently it was Alice who decided on the feature of interest.

Towards the end of the book – the end of the day with Barney – there is a picture of him reading in bed:

Gf	*Barney loves to read at bedtime.*
A	Just like Alice.
Gf	Yes, Alice reads at bedtime.
A	Barney's holding the book.
Gf	He is.
A	Barney's reading.
Gf	I think he likes reading.
A	Yes.

(2 years 8 months)

Books which contain such images of literacy (Hall and Robinson, 1995) are useful. Especially, perhaps, where it is a well known character who is engaged in the reading or writing. But this was not the reason for providing the book about Barney. It was Alice's interests which suggested that she would enjoy seeing Barney in a book as she liked the television character.

Alice continued to enjoy books which featured the important aspects of rhyme, rhythm or repetition of phrases or sentences. Such repetition creates a rhythm within the story. *Good-Night Owl* (Hutchins, 1972) has this quality. Sharing this new book for Alice, we looked first at the cover and the front-piece where the various birds and the squirrel are depicted. Then we started on the text:

Gf	*Owl tried to sleep.*
	The owl's sleeping in the tree isn't it.
A	Yes.
	Owl's got his eyes closed.
Gf	*The bees buzzed,*
	buzz buzz,
	and owl tried to
A	*sleep.*
	There's the buzzy bees.
Gf	It is isn't it.
	The squirrel cracked nuts,
	crunch crunch,
	and owl tried
A	*to sleep.*
Gf	*The crows croaked,*
	caw caw,
	and owl
A	*tried to sleep.*
	There's two crows.
Gf	Yes.
	They're sitting in the tree.
A	Near squirrel.
Gf	Yes.
	The woodpecker pecked,
	rat-a-tat! rat-a-tat!
	and
A	*owl tried to sleep.*

Alice continued to contribute the repetition of *'owl tried to sleep'* until we reached the last two pages when the repetitive story structure alters. The *'and'* announcing the repeat line was sufficient to trigger the response from Alice, once we had read first four pages, to which she had gradually increased her contribution. Inevitably, as soon as the book was finished, Alice insisted it be read again.

On the second reading Alice was ready to do her bit right from the first page:

Gf	*Owl*
A	*tried to sleep.*
Gf	*The bees buzzed,*
	buzz buzz,
	and
A	*owl tried to sleep.*

This time Alice made comments and seemed more interested in the story line and in her contribution. After we finished, Alice decided she would read the book on her own.

Alice wandered off and sat down on the floor with the book on her lap:

A *Owl tried to sleep.*
There's the bees.

Owl tried to sleep
and the bees buzzed
buzz buzz.

Owl tried to sleep
and the squirrel was eating in the tree.
(2 years 9 months)

Alice's reading continued in this way. For each page she provided the key repetitive line of 'owl tried to sleep' and added some comment about the squirrel or bird appearing in the picture. On this third read Alice read or retold the story through to the finish but without the resolution of the story when night falls and all the creatures except the owl go to sleep.

Her desire to read the book on her own coincided with an adult reading, so Alice wanted to read too. She often pretended to read books with or without pictures just as she pretended to drive a car, drink cups of bath-water tea and give imaginary drinks to dolls or toy animals. It is important for young children to see adults reading; Alice was learning about reading partly by adults demonstrating the act of reading.

A few weeks later Alice again opted to read on her own, although initially it looked as though she was going to share a book. She was standing by her collection of books and glancing at the covers:

Gf	Are you going to get a book?
A	Yes.
Gf	What are you getting?
A	A 'Barney' one, I think.
Gf	Okay.
A	At the Farm? (*Barney's Farm Animals* – Kearns and O'Brien, 1993)
Gf	Yes, all right.
A	Or, shall we have Barney waking up? (*A Day with Barney* – Dudko and Larsen, 1994)
Gf	You choose.

Alice collected both books and brought them to me.

A	Which would you prefer?
Gf	*Barney's Farm Animals.*
A	Here it is.

Alice then sat down with the other book in front of her. The clear suggestion was that we were each to read a book.

A	I'm reading on my own.
Gf	You are aren't you.
	Barney is on a farm.
A	*Barney is sleeping. (It's time to wake up, Barney!)*
	Barney's eating his corn flakes. (What are you eating for breakfast, Barney?)
Gf	*'Cock-a-doodle-doo,' says the rooster.*
	Barney says, 'Good morning.'

A   Alice have this one now.

The Barney books were duly exchanged.

A   *Barney is with the cow. ('Moo, moo,' says the cow.)*
        (2 years 10 months)

The dual reading of the Barney books continued for some minutes, the books being exchanged three more times as Alice decided which one she wanted to be reading. Throughout the activity Alice indicated her pleasure at reading by herself – just like the adults she knew.

A few days later Alice demonstrated her growing awareness of environmental print. She was using a measuring tape to measure various objects around the house – or at least she was using the measuring tape in way similar to that which she had observed. This presented a good chance to measure Alice's head for a prospective bicycle helmet. A special tape for that purpose had been collected already, without Alice's knowledge, from TOYS 'R' US (which has the <R> reversed in the logo).

Gm   Here's another measuring tape.
A   Oh. I have it.
        Look TOYS 'R' US.
Gm   It does say TOYS 'R' US doesn't it.

This was by no means the first time Alice had demonstrated recognising a logo graphic but this time the logo was recognised very much out of context – at home rather than at the warehouse, and on a strip of paper rather than as a bold sign. Secondly, the logo on the measuring tape was written in blue on a yellow background, which is quite different from the usual multi-coloured logo of TOYS 'R' US. Perhaps it was the distinctive central reversed letter <R> that enabled Alice to recognise the logo but whatever the case, it demonstrated her developing attention to features of print.

Aspects of the stories which Alice had shared with an adult (e.g. *Good Night Owl*, Hutchins, 1972) often reappeared in her conversations. So, noticing a bird in the silver birch in the back garden, she commented:

A	There's a bird in the white tree.
Gf	Yes, there's a bird in the silver birch tree.
	What kind is it?
A	It's a robin I think.
Gf	It is, It's a robin.
A	*The robin peeped,*
	pip pip,
	and owl tried to sleep.
Gf	He did, didn't he?
	And in the story there was a squirrel.
A	*cracked nuts,*
	crunch crunch,
Gf	He did, the squirrel cracked nuts.
	But we haven't got a squirrel in the tree.
A	No.
	(2 years 11 months)

That Alice used some of the language from a story heard many times is to be expected. Carol Fox (1993) – among others – has shown how children will often use that language, interwoven with language from other sources, to inform their own story telling. Such instances stress the importance of children hearing many stories read and repeated often so that they can develop their repertoire of language and explore words, phrases and discourse patterns.

It was not, however, just with stories that Alice picked up phrases or sentences. One of her favourite TV recordings at the time was a nature programme about dolphins. In it the narrator introduces a variety of sea life and comments about each and once, when he introduced the 'trigger fish' Alice said 'that will blow their cover!' This made sense to the adults in the room only when the narrator then described how the trigger fish would 'blow their (other creatures') cover' in order to expose those sheltering under the sand, and so find food.

The same TV programme demonstrated Alice's growing awareness of print and her interest in finding out about it. It begins with two captions appearing separately on the screen:

A	What's that?
Gf	It says

> *Baywatch*

A	What's that now?
Gf	*a dolphin's view*

It tells us that the programme is about dolphins.

A	And dugong.
Gf	We will see a dugong, yes.
A	What are those letters?
Gf	It tells us who is going to do the talking. It says

> *Narrated by*
> *David Attenborough*

So David Attenborough is going to tell us about all the different creatures.

> *Narrated by*
> *David Attenborough*

A	Yes.

(2 years 11 months)

This exchange indicated clearly Alice's capacity to distinguish between pictures and print. This was also evident in her drawings and writing. Her drawings could usually be recognised as such. Her writing alongside them would demonstrate, typically, linearity and pseudoletters. In the week before her third birthday, Alice wrote clearly and unequivocally a number of letters: too

and she announced:

A   A <t> and two <o>'s.

Alice was drawing on a magnetic chalk board and placing magnetic letters on it while from time to time asking about them. Then she did her drawing and wrote the three letters on a piece of paper.

Alice continued to enjoy nursery rhymes. She listened frequently to a CD recording of *50 Favourite Nursery Rhymes and Songs* (Early Learning Centre, 1995) and many of the rhymes had to be repeated constantly until Alice could join in with her favourite rhymes. But it

Picture 11:Alice writing 't' on her chalkboard. 2 years 11 months.

was stories which were the major contact point with print. And, probably because Alice had acquired a bicycle at Christmas, the story *Topsy and Tim ride their bikes* (Adamson and Adamson, 1992) became a favourite for a few weeks. The story reflects the difficulty of learning to ride and the need for stabiliser wheels, as well as helping parents to emphasise the need for children to wear protective helmets:

Gf   *'Easy peasy,' said Topsy.*
          But it wasn't. Learning how to
          balance was quite difficult.

          Topsy and Tim kept falling off.
          'I can see you're going to need
          the helmets I bought,' said Mummy.

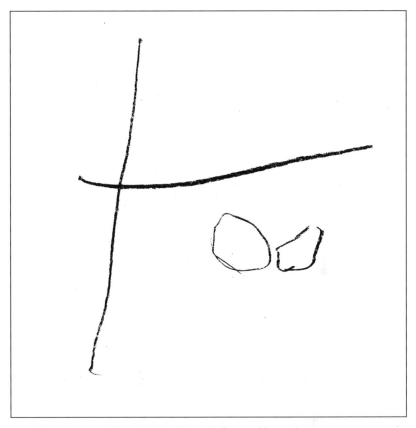

Figure 3: A t and two o's. 2 years 11 months.

A   Topsy needs to wear a helmet.
Gf   Yes, just like you.
A   I've got a Skid Lid.
Gf   You have, yes. Your helmet is a Skid Lid.
       (2 years 11 months)

Alice frequently wanted to hear this story, which she and her father had chosen from the supermarket. And she was content just to listen to it – only rarely did she make any comment. Perhaps there were so many words in this text that she just needed to listen in order to absorb the words. This was also true of another favourite at this time – *Alfie*

Gets in First (Hughes, 1981) – where Alice abandoned her normal questioning as she listened repeatedly to the lengthy story. Alice also used some of the language from the book in her everyday activities – any activity she engaged in became, for a few days, 'easy peasy'.

Alice at 3 years old

Alice remained enthusiastic about books and the sharing of them with an adult. There were collections of books for her to look at home and at her grandparents' house. She also visited the local library to borrow books – and often had to be coaxed to leave.

A review of her involvement with print, her own initiated literacy activities and her shared story readings indicated a range of literacy knowledge at three years of age. These are listed below.

During the shared story readings, Alice:
>asked questions about the text,
>commented on the text and illustrations,
>responded to those texts which asked questions,
>recognised the role of print by pointing to, and saying, certain words,
>noted that characters in texts also read,
>requested frequent repeat readings,
>memorised and contributed to parts of the repeat readings.

Alice watched TV, during which she:
>acquired words and phrases,
>recognised the concluding captions as signalling the end,
>wanted to talk about the print on the screen.

In her response to environmental print Alice recognised:
>key logos in context,
>logos out of their normal context,
>some logos out of context and in different colours.

Other aspects of literacy were evident. Alice:
>differentiated between drawing and her writing,

recognised some letters and named them,
wrote a few letters and named them,
attempted to write her own forename,
tapped the keyboard of a computer,
shared in the singing of nursery rhymes,
vocalised and copied sound rhymes.

Alice used her experience of the shared story readings to:
acquire words, phrases or sentences,
use those words, phrases and sentences in other contexts,
memorise complete short stories,
play at reading to herself and to her toys animals,
organise her dolls with newspapers for reading,
read to her baby sister.

Clearly, reading and writing experiences were an important part of Alice's life. Other events were also important for her. Three weeks before her second birthday her sister Caitlin was born. And on the day before her third birthday she helped her Mum, Dad and Caitlin to move to a new house.

Chapter 5
From 3 to 4 years

On Alice's third birthday it snowed. So we set off on a long walk across frozen fields and left time for only a brief visit to the library to return books and borrow new ones. One of the books that Alice chose, mainly because she liked the front cover, was *Jasper's Jungle Journey* (Biro, 1995). Once back home, she had to have the book read to her. At the end of the first reading, which took place largely without any comment from Alice, she said:

A   Read it again.

'Read it again' are the very words used by Cecilia at 3 years 2 months when she listened to her mother reading a story (Payton, 1984). Young children like to have frequent repeat readings of a book so they can get to know the text. *Jasper's Jungle Journey* was read to Alice, at her request, eight times over. With each reading Alice made more comments about the story or joined in with some of the words e.g.

F   *A lion*
A   *wearing purple socks.*

And later in Jasper's journey as he looked for his teddy:

F   *A rhino*
A   *with an enormous horn.*

Such repeat readings, and the regular return to other of her favourite stories were a feature of Alice's contact with books at this age. She took great pleasure in knowing a story and joining in the reading.

One of the books to which Alice still returned regularly and enthu-siastically was *Good-Night Owl*. By now she had almost entirely memorised it, so when we read it together Alice contributed more to the reading than I did, although I acted as a guide through the book:

Gf	*Owl*
A	*tried to sleep.*
Gf	*The*
A	*bees buzzed,*
	buzz buzz,
	and owl tried to sleep.
Gf	*The squirrel*
A	*cracked nuts*
	crunch crunch,
	and owl tried to sleep.
	(3 years)

There were important differences from when we first shared this book: Alice's substantial contribution to the reading; her memory of the text and the sequence of the story; her lack of comment during the reading; and her enjoyment – perhaps of being in control of the story. After we had read the whole story, Alice turned back to the beginning, possibly with the intention of rereading, but the title page led her from the story:

A	I think they're all there.
Gf	Yes, I think so.
A	Owl's sitting in an <o>.
Gf	Yes, and there's some other <o>s there as well.
A	Squirrel's on one.
Gf	And, I think the crows are on another.
	What else can you see?
A	The sparrow's on a <t>.
Gf	Mm.
A	That one is upside down (pointing to the exclamation mark).
Gf	It does look like an upside down letter.
A	The robin's going pip, pip.
	(3 years)

Alice drew attention to a punctuation mark which she saw as an 'upside down' letter, indicating the close attention that she now gave to print and her ability to discriminate specific aspects of it. She would now often write 'a big <A>' on a sheet of paper – an important letter for her as she moved towards writing her own name.

Alice continued to memorise substantial parts of the books and stories that she had induced adults to 'read again'. One of the books which Caitlin was currently enjoying was *Rosie and Jim: Going for a Walk* (Ragdoll Productions, 1995), and often when an adult read it for Caitlin, Alice would be listening and looking at the illustrations. The extent of her real involvement emerged when she started to join with the adult in the reading. Eventually, after numerous readings, Alice waited only for the first page to be read before she recited the rest.

M   *Jim and Rosie went out walking, and*
            what did they see?

A   *Ten flowers dancing*
            Nine rabbits hopping
            Eight chickens hatching
            Seven children chatting
            Six squirrels scuttling
            Five sailing boats
            Four flying kites
            Three brown cows
            Two scarecrows

            And one Duck
            quacking time for tea.
            (3 years 1 month)

Her accurate recitation or part-singing to the tune of 'Five gold rings' was usually aided by glancing at each page but at times Alice sang through the book while playing at something else.

From time to time Alice and Caitlin would sit near each other and look at books. Alice could now recall the words of a number of books and

Picture 12: Alice and Caitlin reading books. 3 years.

this meant that she could behave like an independent reader even though she could not read the conventional print on each page. It also meant that on occasions she was able to 'read' short books to her younger sister:

A   *I wrote to the zoo*
          to send me a pet.
          They sent me an
C   (Pulls the flap open)
A   Elephant
          He was too big!
          I sent him back.
          (3 years 1 month)

Alice could read *Dear Zoo* (Campbell, 1982) by recalling the many readings she had heard. And she had noted the behaviour of the adult during such readings, as shown by her comment to Caitlin that it was an elephant, before she carried on with the reading.

There were other readings where Alice behaved very much as the listener, especially with books that were new to her and for which there could be no expectation of her reading or recalling the text. With some new books she would not even comment, ask a question, or connect with her own experiences. Instead, she wanted to hear the story read several times in succession as happened with *The Park in the Dark* (Waddell, 1989) borrowed from the local library.

Only after the whole book was read did Alice say anything – and that was to request that it be read again. Perhaps Alice thought that reading involved memorising the whole book so that it could be read to others!

Paddington Bear is a much loved character and Alice had a toy Paddington in her collection. Although the original books by Michael Bond are quite lengthy, there are a number of adaptations or miniature versions. One little hardboard book is *Paddington has a Bath* (Bond, 1992a). Alice was introduced to it at this time and as soon as the reading began Alice started commenting on the story and pictures.

Gf	*Paddington*
	needs a bath.
A	Because he's got very dirty.
Gf	He has got dirty.
	He fills the
	bath
A	He's got too much.
Gf	It's running over isn't it?
	and jumps in.
A	Splash.
Gf	Splash.
	What bubbles!

At this point Alice, for whatever reason, decided to listen to the rest in silence. Only when the last page was reached did she make another comment.

Gf *Oh dear,*
   Paddington
   needs a bath.

A He's got dirty again.
Gf He has, he needs another bath.
  (3 years 2 months)

The Paddington story was read for the first time just before bedtime and, because it was new, it had to accompany Alice to bed. Next morning Alice showed me how she had internalised the story.

Gf I can see your new Paddington book.
A Yes.
Gf So what did Paddington get up to?
A He needed a bath,
  and he spilt some water,
  and washed his hat.
  Paddington made a mess with the toothpaste.
  He went to the shelf and made another mess,
  and had to have a bath again.
Gf Why did he need a bath in the first place?
A 'Cos he got dirty playing football.
  (3 years 2 months)

Although there was no mention of football in the text, the picture with a football beside a very dirty Paddington does suggest that he had 'got dirty playing football'. Alice's account of what Paddington does is entirely accurate.

As well as reading, Alice continued to enjoy drawing and some of her drawings, often accompanied by writing, added to our understanding of her thinking about print. Her drawing of grandma was based on an oval with blue hair: 'Cos I haven't got grey,' and her writing on three pseudoletters. As she wrote the three shapes she indicated that they were:

Alice   Camp   bell

Linking the three shapes to her forename and the syllables in her surname demonstrated some understanding of the sounds that she heard and an attempt to represent these sounds on the page.

A week later her writing alongside the pictures she drew on five sheets of paper was somewhat different. This time she wrote what she said was 'Alice' on each sheet. Each 'signature' contained an <A>, four of them with the <A> as the first letter. All contained the letters <l> and <i>, and in four of these the <i> followed on directly from the <l>. The other letter shapes included <o>, <t>, and half-moon shapes in various orientations which might have been attempts to produce the <c> and <e> of her name (3 years 3 months). In all Alice produced three sheets with four letters, one with five and one with six. Alice was clearly developing her knowledge of literacy. Later she wrote 'Alloo' on the back of a card 'to grandad' – although 'gd' had to suffice for grandad.

Alice also kept returning to nursery rhymes. She and Caitlin enjoyed dancing to the recordings of rhymes and Alice would generally join in with the words. 'A lift-the-flap-book' of rhymes – *Hey Diddle Diddle and Other Mother Goose Rhymes* – (Rayner, 1995) became an attraction for Alice, and for Caitlin when she had a chance.

Gf   You know this one.
A   *Humpty Dumpty*
            Sat on a wall,
            Humpty Dumpty
            Had a great fall;
         (Turns the flap)
            All the King's horses
            And all the King's men
            Couldn't put Humpty
            Together again.
         Look Caitlin there's Humpty all broken.

Figure 4: A card to grandad. 3 years 3 months.

(Turns two pages)
This is a funny one.

Gf   Are you going to read it to Caitlin? (Actually to ask if Alice was going to recite the rhyme which she knew well.)

A   *Hey diddle diddle,*
            The cat and the fiddle,
            The cow jumped over the moon;
            The little dog laughed,
            To see such fun,
            And the dish ran away
            With the spoon.

That's silly.
The dish ran away with the spoon?

Gf   It is a strange one, isn't it.

(3 years 3 months)

Evidence suggests that the ability of young children to explore and enjoy such rhymes will eventually contribute to their reading development because they acquire an awareness of phonology (Meek, 1990). For the moment the sheer pleasure of playing with the words was reason enough to encourage the continuing exploration of the rhymes.

After finishing a shared reading of a book some days later, Alice took the book and sat on the floor.

Alice   I'm going to read now.

Gm   Okay, you read it.

Such invitations as 'you read it' had up to now been followed by Alice reciting the book from memory. It may have been her increased awareness of the role of the print in books that led her to a different conclusion this time.

Alice   I don't know how to do it.

Gm   I've heard you reading that book.

Alice   I'll use your glasses.

          (3 years 4 months)

Alice then proceeded to look through the book with the aid of her grandmother's reading glasses. Did Alice think that it was the glasses that enabled her grandmother to make sense of the print?

What was evident was that Alice was beginning to recognise some of the words in the books that she read, and perhaps that made her realise that she didn't know how to read all the words. With *Good-Night Owl* (Hutchins, 1972) she delighted in looking for the word 'owl' – and finding it on each page. She also enjoyed looking for <o> and <A> in magazines and newspapers and would immediately announce that there was the <o> for owl, or the <A> for Alice. She also requested to have 'Alice' written on a sheet of paper, then 'owl', 'mummy' and 'Barney' (which was now one of Caitlin's favourite characters). Alice would then tell adults about these four significant words, pointing to them and naming them. She became able to recognise certain words just as she developed the writing of her name – which now started always with the three letters <A> <l> <i>, followed by two other letter shapes with some similarity to the letters <c> <e>.

But mainly it was reading books with an adult which Alice liked best. She was enthusiastic about a board version of *The Very Hungry Caterpillar* (Carle, 1969). First, she had to have the book read to her and typically demanded that I 'Read it again'. It was only after the third reading that she began to make comments and ask questions as the book was read, and these were wide ranging:

Alice   Why has the sun got a face?
Where's the caterpillar going?
I like strawberries.
What's a stomach ache?
He should eat leaves all the time.
What's a cocoon?

After those first few readings Alice began to complete the story by reciting the final page.

Alice   *he was a beautiful butterfly!*
(3 years 4 months)

Subsequently, Alice decided that we had to hunt for caterpillars in the garden. Unfortunately, none could be found although a number of leaves with holes in them suggested that caterpillars had been dining there.

Within a few weeks, Alice had perfected the <c > <e> in her name, and now whenever she wrote it – which she did frequently during the course of a day – she did so in a conventional format. She had also absorbed the key phrase from *The Very Hungry Caterpillar* 'but he was still hungry'. So during a sharing of the book she contributed this phrase to the reading, as well as making other comments:

Gf   *On Monday*
he ate through
one apple.
A   *But he was still*
hungry.

Gf	*On Tuesday*
	he ate through
	two pears,
A	*but he was*
	still hungry.
Gf	*On Wednesday*
	he ate through
	three plums,
A	I'm three.
Gf	You are three years old.
	but
A	*he was still*
	hungry.
Gf	*On Thursday*
	he ate through
	four strawberries
	but
A	*he was still*
	hungry
	I like strawberries.
Gf	You do don't you.
A	I'll be four soon.
Gf	Well, you will in a while, on your next birthday.
	(3 years 5 months)

The phrase 'but he was still hungry' had captured her attention. But there was also food to be talked about and certain numbers led to brief diversions to consider the important features of her age and forthcoming birthday.

Ten Little Bears (Roffey, 1993) was another book she enjoyed at this time. The first two pages read:

> *Ten little Teddy Bears*
> *sitting down to dine,*
> *One didn't like the soup*
> *and then there were nine.*

The page configuration encourages children to take part in the story. Alice particularly liked to look for the Teddy Bear on the previous page who was next to drop out. Inevitably also it led to counting down from ten to one as well as counting from one to ten.

A book that Alice had heard frequently at home was *Sly Fox and Red Hen* (Hunia, 1993). This is one of a collection of traditional and popular stories, shortened and simplified for young readers – but still telling a real story. Because of its clear short story line with supporting pictures Alice soon memorised much of it and then took great delight in reading it to an audience:

Alice   *Here is Red Hen.*
      Her home is in
      a tree.
      This is Sly Fox.
      He wants to eat
      Red Hen.
      I will go and look
      for her (Red Hen),
      says the Sly Fox (he says).
      (3 years 6 months)

There were some deviations from the text but Alice was able to behave like a reader – and appear to behave just like the adults she knew.

Incidental encounters with print were frequent and diverse. Noticing two jars on the table she asked:

A   Does that say
     Honey?
Gf   Yes, that's
     Honey.
A   Pooh likes honey.
Gf   He does doesn't he?
A   What does that say?
Gf   *Pure Set*

And that's
Sainsbury's.

A   There's
Sainsbury's
again.

Gf   Yes that's
Sainsbury's.
But this isn't Honey, this is
Black currant
Jam.

A   Is that one
Jam.

Gf   Good girl, yes that's
Jam.

Alice was inquisitive about words and letters, and often asked questions of the adults in her vicinity. A few days later I was checking out a route for a forthcoming car journey and after a few moments, Alice came and looked over my shoulder:

A   What's that?

Gf   A book.

A   It's not a reading book.

Gf   Isn't it? What is it then?

A   (Pause)

Gf   What book is it?

A   It's a which way you're going book.

'A which way you're going book' seemed a fair description of the gazetteer of maps. This showed that Alice was recognising that print was the key feature in a book. Alice again showed her attention to print when she wrote a shopping list with her name at the top.

At bed-time Alice liked to have a story telling. And if her Grandma put her to bed then it had to be a Topsy and Tim story but not a specific one from a familiar book – any tale would do as long as it was about them. Alice's interest in these characters extended to being able to

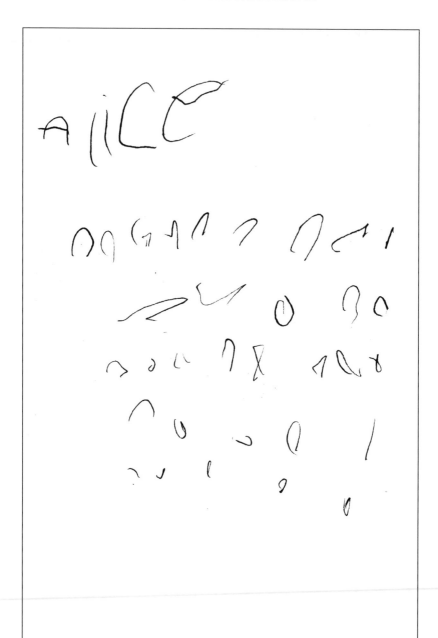

Figure 5: Own name and shopping list. 3 years 6 months.

recognise their names, so when a new book, *Topsy and Tim meet the ambulance crew* (Adamson and Adamson, 1996), was read to her for the first time, she could join in at once:

Gm	*When Topsy and*
A	*Tim*
Gm	*arrived at school,*
	they saw a big, white ambulance standing
	in the school playground.
	'Oh dear,' said
A	*Mummy.*
Gm	*'I hope there*
	hasn't been an accident.'
	'It's all right Mum,' said
A	*Tim.*
	(3 years 7 months)

The first 'Tim' that Alice read was linked to 'Topsy and', so was easy to guess without looking. But the subsequent contributions from Alice of 'mummy' and 'Tim' were less predictable and might well have been words which she could recognise.

It is not unusual for children to be interested in other books by an author whose work they have enjoyed. Alice selected one of Dr Seuss's books, *Green Eggs and Ham* (Seuss, 1960) when she visited the local library with her father and then wanted it read to her.

F	*...I do not like*
	that Sam-I-am!
	Do you like
	green eggs and ham?
	(3 years 8 months)

The book continues in the same vein with sixty two pages of rhyme, and young children enjoy the flow of words, the rhyme and the nonsense. After listening to the whole book, Alice asked for it to be read again! She also wanted to know:

A   Where does it say green eggs?

Her interest in particular words was also apparent when she sat at the computer, at home with her father or when visiting her grandfather. Her understanding of parts of the process of writing on the computer led her to ask for a list of words including: egg, Sam, and ham from the recent story as well as mummy, daddy and Caitlin, and she happily tapped in 'Alice' all by herself. Then she had to have the list of words printed so that she could show it to whoever was around. She also used these words to guide her naming of the pictures she drew.

Then Alice found another Dr Seuss nonsense rhyme book, *Hop on Pop* (Seuss, 1963) which she had read to her at home by her mother or father and then wanted read by others:

Gf	*Pup in cup*
	Cup on pup
	Mouse on
A	*house*
Gf	*House on*
A	*mouse*
	We all are tall.
	We all are small.
	I'll count them.
Gf	Go on then.
A	One, two, three, four, five, six, seven, eight.
Gf	There are eight, aren't there?
	We
A	*all play ball*
Gf	*up on a wall.*
	Fall off the wall
A	*We play all day.*
	We fight all night.
Gf	*He is after me.*
	Jim is
A	*after him.*
	(3 years 8 months)

Figure 6: Alice and Caitlin. 3 years 8 months/

During these readings Alice listened, made comments and then counted the eight figures on one page. She also read the pages or parts of pages she had memorised and which were significant to her and provided the final few words to some sentences. All this made Alice look like a reader, and perhaps she felt like one too, but she was largely recalling the words rather than reading them.

Alice's interest in recognising certain words became so strong that at times it appeared to distract her from the story. Reading through *Paddington Goes Shopping* (Bond, 1992b) for the umpteenth time, she suddenly noticed an <s> in eggs:

Gf   *He finds the fruit*
              and the vegetables
              and the eggs.

A   Why has egg got an \<s\>?

Gf   Well, how many are there in this picture?

A   One, two, three, four, five, six.

Gf   That's right.
              So it says eggs not egg.

A   Yes, eggs.
              (3 years 9 months)

Another time, looking through her collection of books on her own, she carefully examined the front and back covers of *Zoo Animals* (Butterfield, 1995), then brought it over to me:

A   Look there's 'and' and 'zoo'.

Gf   Yes, that says 'and' and that word is 'zoo'.
              It's a book about Zoo Animals, isn't it.

A   Mmh, I like the Hippo best.

Gf   That hippo gets all muddy, doesn't it?
              (3 years 9 months)

Whenever Alice drew a picture she liked to write her name on the paper – 'So you know who did it' – and label the drawing:

A   How do you write Whale?

Gm   \<W\>, \<h\>, \<a\>, \<l\>, \<e\>. (each later named).

For a very few drawings Alice could now add her own accurate writing. Under her picture of an owl she wrote the word 'owl' without any help. The word owl was one of the words in her collection that she liked to see on the computer screen and often which asked to have printed out 'like daddy and grandad do'.

Both Alice and Caitlin were enjoying *We're Not Tired* (Young, 1994) at this time and both liked to provide the finish to a sentence. On the first page Alice spoke the last word in the first two sentences, then a more extensive part of the sentence on the last line:

Figure 7: A snake. 3 years 9 months.

F   *'Hello, I'm Ness and this is my brother,*
A   *Hamish.*
F   *It's bedtime and we've put on our*
A   *pyjamas.*
F   *Mum's come to tuck us in and*
A   *turn out the light.*

More extensive utterance of part of the sentence was also evident later:

F   *So we*
A   *ring and we rose right round the room.*
F   *We go*
A   *huffing and puffing...*
          And dancing and prancing...
          And trumpeting and tooting.
          (3 years 10 months)

While Alice read this last sentence, she followed the writing with her finger. When she reached 'and' she indicated clearly that this was a word she recognised but she had probably memorised the other words as part of the story. Alice confirmed her knowledge of the word 'and' by tapping it on to her list on the computer.

Why did Alice add 'and' in her collection of words when all the rest were names of people, animals or objects? The complete list of words was: Barney, owl, mummy, daddy, Alice, Caitlin, egg, Sam, ham, fox, Topsy and Tim, zoo, and, whale, dolphin, Paddington, bath, glasses. The addition of 'and' had occurred as Alice talked about her collection:

A   That's Alice and Caitlin.
Gf   That's right.
        Where's mummy.
A   There and daddy.
Gf   That's right.
A   Where does it say and?
Gf   You haven't got and there, have you?
A   No.
        Write and.

So 'and' was added for practical reasons whereas the other words were what Sylvia Ashton-Warner (1963) described as organic vocabulary, which would be recognised and remembered. They were words of real meaning for the child.

Her interest in certain special words and her ability to recognise them meant that Alice could make a contribution to the reading of the simple forty-five word text, *Paddington has a bath* which she had shared many times before.

Gm	You know what this book is about.
A	Paddington.
Gm	And what does he do.
A	He has a bath.
Gm	Shall we read it together?
	(pointing at each word)
A	*Paddington*
Gm	*needs*
A	*a bath.*
Gm	*He fills the*
A	*bath*
	and jumps in.
Gm	*What bubbles!*
	(3 years 10 months)

Alice took great pleasure in being able to read parts of this book. In the first three pages, Alice read four words – Paddington, bath, bath, and – at various points, then added three more: a, jump, in. She said these words as part of her memorisation of the book, or in the case of 'a' perhaps as part of her wider knowledge of how language works. Alice was now able to recognise and read some of the words in the book.

Alice continued to want to have new books read to her several times over initially, and made her usual request after *The Very Lonely Firefly* (Carle, 1995) was read to her. However, within a few pages of starting the second reading, at the point where the lonely firefly searched for other fireflies, Alice interrupted with a comment on the story:

A   It will find the other fireflies on the last page. Then it won't be lonely anymore.

And when we reached the final page she said at once:

A   There's all its friends.
      (3 years 11 months)

When Alice did some writing now she generally produced a string of letters which appeared to be random, although some could be linked to words. She always wrote her own name conventionally and Caitlin as a string of letters beginning with a <C>. A picture of 'Humpty Dumpty sat on the wall' included a caption of:

     lHOi wll

The 'wll' at the end of her string of letters was separated from the others by a clear gap and might well have been her attempt at 'wall'. Certainly, she could recognise letters, name them and produce them. On the same day she wrote:

     A B c D e F g h i
     (3 years 11 months)

on her own before moving off to do something else.

Alice at 4 years old

Alice continued to enjoy books. She also looked at print in other contexts and now wrote in a way which clearly distinguished her writing from her drawings. Some of the significant features of her literacy development by the time she reached her fourth birthday were:

During shared readings Alice:
     wanted the story repeated frequently,
     enjoyed contributing the concluding words in a phrase,
     liked to contribute memorable phrases,
     memorised substantial parts of texts,
     sometimes memorised complete stories,
     commented upon aspects of the narrative,

Figure 8: Humpty Dumpty sat on the wall. 3 years 11 months.

asked questions about characters, objects and actions,
recalled stories and occasionally added aspects from the
illustrations,
linked the story to her own environment,
expressed her feelings about stories.

Looking at print, Alice:
commented upon punctuation,
talked about letters,
looked for specific letters in books, newspapers and other
print,
read some key words in environmental print,
recognised other genres such as a gazetteer of maps,
noted the <s> as a plural on a word,
recognised some key words in print e.g. and, owl, zoo.

As Alice developed her writing, she:
produced writing linked to the number of syllables in a line,
developed the writing of her own name from A to Alice,
used a computer to create a small list of known words,
wrote the start of the alphabet from <a> to <i>,
wrote her sister's name as a collection of letters beginning
with <C>.

Chapter 6
From 4 to 5 years

After Alice's fourth birthday it became increasingly difficult to record all the changes and growth in her literacy development. In the course of a few days after Alice turned four I noted a number of literacy events. First, she was sitting at a table and producing some pictures. Then, without any indication that she intended to change from drawing to writing she wrote on a fresh piece of paper 'owl':

A   I've done owl.
Gf   You have you've written owl haven't you.
A   It's like – and owl tried to sleep.
Gf   Yes, just like in that book.

Alice had made the connection from her writing to the story *Good-Night Owl*. Inevitably story readings were still a part of her day and Alice enjoyed listening to *Time for bed NED* (Zinnemann-Hope, 1986) and then reading parts of the book to others:

Gm   What's happening here?
A   His mummy's calling him.
Gm   She is, she's saying....
A   *'Ned.'*
Gm   She is, and now....
A   *'Ned!' 'Ned!' 'Ned!' 'Ned!'*
         'Time for bed, Ned.'
         There's a dog and a cat as well.
Gm   There is isn't there.
A   *'No (Oh) no!' said-Ned said.*

Gm   Yes that's right.
            'Oh no!' Ned said.
            I don't think he wants to go to bed do you?

A   No, but now his mummy's got him.
            'Ned! Bed,
            What's that?

Gm   That's

                I

A   *I said.'*

Gm   Yes.
            'Ned! Bed, I said.'
            (4 years)

As ever, it was difficult to determine fully the extent to which Alice was reading the words or reciting from memory. Nevertheless, her intonation, her apparent close scrutiny of words, and her occasional use of a finger under the words suggested that she was trying to follow the print. This was confirmed later that day:

A   Write something for me.

Gf   What do you want me to write?

A   Something for me to read.

Gf   Okay.
            Alice and Caitlin go to bed.

Two of those words, 'go' and particularly 'bed' play a prominent part in the *Time for bed NED* story, and the others were words that she would know well.

A   **Alice and Caitlin go to bed**.

Gf   That's it.
            Alice and Caitlin go to bed.

Alice was able to read the short sentence she had not seen before, which suggested that her reading of the book had indeed involved close perusal of the print. She was reading parts of the book rather than reciting from memory.

After reading this Alice announced that it was too early to go to bed:

A   Not yet I'm not.
Gf   No, its not time for bed yet is it?
A   I'll do some writing.
Gf   Go on then.
A   *ouvHit*
         What's that say?
Gf   You read it to me.
A   *Ruby*
         Where's the <b>?
Gf   I don't know.
A   I need a <b>.
         <b>
         I'll do some more.
         ovmuA
Gf   What does that one say?
A   *Kipper – Kipper*
         I need a <p> for Kipper.
Gf   I think you do.
A   *<p>*
         Alice to o
         That's not a good <o>.
         owl
Gf   I think I know that one.
A   What is it?
Gf   *Alice to*
A   *owl*
Gf   That's lovely.
         Alice to owl.
         Just like in a birthday card.
         (4 years)

Alice's attempts at writing revealed that she recognised certain letters and could reproduce them in her writing and that she was hearing some of the sounds in words and linking them to particular letters.

Alice's phonemic awareness enabled her to recognise the need for a <b>, then a <p> in the two words that she constructed. [Kipper is the character in a picture book by Mick Inkpen (1991)]. Thirdly, she demonstrated that she could recall a number of words and write them in an accurate form.

Her latest favourite book was *Do You Want to Be My Friend?* (Carle, 1988). The adventures of the mouse as it tries to find a friend, delights young children. The layout of the book encourages the child to predict the next animal – especially on the first reading. And the repetition, which is used for a real purpose, is soon learnt. So after having the book read to her at least four times she decided to read it to her sister.

A   The mouse is asking,
> *'Do you want to be my friend?'*
> *But the horse says, No. It's eating the grass.*
> *('No,' said the brown horse, eating the grass.)*

C   It's a horse.

A   *So the mouse ran on.*
> *'Do you want to be my friend?'*
> *The crocodile says, No. It's got a bird on its back.*
> *('No,' said the crocodile with the bird on her back.)*
> (4 years 1 month)

Alice continued to read to the end of the book, her memory producing an accurate and conventional reading of the two lines which appear on every alternate page. Her recall of the story, aided by the pictures, enabled her to produce a meaningful, although not fully accurate, reading of the lines about the different animals.

When Alice returned to this book a few days later she read the line 'Do you want to be my friend?' very deliberately, pointing to each of the words as she read it. This suggested that she could now read those words or, if she was relying on her memory that she understood that each word was surrounded by space and that each written word could be spoken. Above all, the sisters were thoroughly enjoying the story, and Caitlin was soon joining in with the 'Do you want to be my friend?' repetition as Alice read.

It's My Birthday (Oxenbury, 1993) became a new favourite a few weeks later. As usual, Alice's reaction was to want to have the book read to her a number of times before she became more involved as the reader and wanted to read it to others.

A   Can I read this to you?

Gm   Of course you can Alice.

A   *It's My Birthday* (pointing with her finger to each word)

                But what does that say Grandma?

Gm   It's the name of the lady who wrote it.

                She's the author, Helen Oxenbury.

A   That's the hen getting the eggs (a picture page without words).

                  'It's My Birthday and
                  I'm going to make a cake.' (pointing to the words).

Gm   Good girl.

A   *'It's My Birthday and*
                  I'm going to make a cake.
                  I need some eggs.'
                  'I'll get you some eggs,'
                  said the chicken.

                Look the bear's playing with the ball.

                  'It's My Birthday and
                  I'm going to make a cake.
                  I 've got the eggs.'
                What's this Grandma?

Gm   What letter does it start with?

A   *<B>*

Gm   */Bu/*

A   *But I need some*
                What's that Grandma?

Gm   *flour*

A   *flour.'*
                  'I'll get you some flour,'
                  said the bear. (4 years 2 months)

Alice read with confidence from the book, following each word with her finger and asking for help when she needed it. Even if she was reading from memory rather than from the print, she followed the print word for word with her finger. And she recognised that there were words of which she was unsure. Alice was able to read through to the end of the book like this, aided by the key repeat sentences which the author had made an integral part of the narrative. 'It's my birthday and I'm going to make a cake' was the first sentence on each page except the last two. Such repeats help young readers in their reading and, as in this story, they are intrinsic to the story structure.

Alice also enjoyed playing with words at odd moments in the day. Chukovsky (1963) suggested that playing with words links to children's interest in creating rhymes. When Alice read *It's My Birthday* on one occasion, she was diverted by the cat getting some butter and milk:

A   *'I'll get you some butter and milk,'*
            said the cat.
            The cat sat on the bricks not on a mat.
            cat, sat, mat, hat.
Gf   Yes, they're all alike, aren't they?
A   And bat and fat
            (4 years 2 months)

Alice's awareness of words with the same rime and different onset letters demonstrated both her interest in words and her developing knowledge or phonemic awareness about them. It is this feature of rhyming, this awareness of onset and rime, that Goswami and Bryant (1990) believe to be of such significance in children's development as readers. Alice was learning about these linguistic features incidentally, as she enjoyed books and talked with adults about them.

Alice continued to ask for new books to be reread, often several times. Confronted with *Slinki Malinki, Open the Door* (Dodd, 1993), she wanted to hear it read through, contribute one or two words on the second reading and then play a progressively bigger part in the later readings. A key repeated page describes how Slinki Malinki swings on a door handle in order to open the door and Alice heard this six times during the first reading. The construction of the words on the page naturally pulls children into the book and by the second reading Alice was ready to say the key words at the end of the line:

Gf	*Slinki Malinki*
	jumped high off the
A	*floor,*
Gf	*he swung on a*
A	*handle*
Gf	*and opened*
A	*a door.*

By the third reading, all on one evening, Alice was contributing the major part of this verse:

Gf	*Slinki Malinki*
	jumped
A	*high off the floor,*
Gf	*he*
A	*swung on a handle*
Gf	*and*
A	*opened*
	a door.

(4 years 3 months)

Alice was prepared to listen to the adventures of Slinky Malinki and Stickybeak Syd on the other pages but in all later readings the linking page was recited in full by Alice. Such books capture the attention of young children, and the rhythm and rhyme allows them to participate. This book also enticed Alice, briefly, to try to swing on a door handle as she role-played parts of the story!

In the next few weeks I noted three interesting aspects relating to Alice's contact with books. First, she returned to the sentence that she had me write some months before – a sentence that had now been extended into a small rhyme. Alice enjoyed reading word by word this eight word rhyme. Partly because it related to her and Caitlin, but perhaps also because she could read every word:

A   *Alice and Caitlin*
        go to bed
        go to bed
        go to bed.
        Alice and Caitlin
        go to bed
        Grandad said.
        (4 years 4 months)

This lead to a number of similar rhymes being requested by Alice. They had to have the same attributes, namely to be short, to relate to her actions, and to be made up of words she could read. She asked for the following rhyme to be written, which she then read:

A   *Alice and Caitlin*
        go to the swings
        go to the swings
        go to the swings.
        Alice and Caitlin
        go to the swings
        Alice and daddy said.

Later that same day she wrote her own rhyme:

        Alice ooz
        Alice to zoo
        Alice said.

Zoo was written with the <z> at the end of the word in the first line, but in front of the two <o>s in the second. Alice also asked about the word 'said'. She was looking closely at words and enjoyed being able to read each one.

Secondly, Alice maintained her enthusiasm for shared readings of books, where she took great pleasure in the flow of words as the narrative unfolded. Another book by Lynley Dodd, *Hairy Maclary from Donaldson's Dairy* (Dodd, 1983) became a particular favourite. The dog Hairy Maclary goes for a walk and gradually other dogs join in. This group of dogs became part of Alice's language and memorised the whole cast without looking at the words (as could Caitlin whenever she got the chance):

A   *Schnitzel von Krumm*
             with a very low tum,
             Blitzer Maloney
             all skinny and bony,
             Muffin McLay
             like a bundle of hay,
             Bottomley Potts
             covered in spots,
             Hercules Morse
             as big as a horse
      (4 years 4 months)

A third incident highlighted Alice's recall of enjoyable stories. Alice was looking at some animal pictures with her Grandmother:

Gm   There's another animal from Australia.
A   Koala.
Gm   It is a Koala, isn't it?
A   Yes.
       Koala Lou, I do love you.

This sentence comes from *Koala Lou* by Mem Fox (1988) and had become part of Alice's language repertoire. Story readings were continuing to contribute to Alice's knowledge of the world and to her language.

A division between reading the words in a story and reading the story remained evident. When Alice returned to the book *Time for bed NED* she read deliberately and slowly because the simple text and her knowledge of some words enabled her to achieve a successful conventional read. Alice was sitting alone and began to read aloud but brought me into the reading with questions:

A	*'Ned.'*
	'Ned!' 'Ned!' 'Ned!' 'Ned!'
	Grandad what does that say?
Gf	*Time*
A	*'Time for bed, Ned.'*
	(pause)
Gf	*Oh*
A	*'Oh no!' Ned said.*
	'Ned! Bed,
Gf	*I*
A	*I said.'*
Gf	Yes.
A	*'No. Not Bed.'*
	What's that one?
Gf	*Come*
A	*'Come on, Ned.'*
	'No!'
	What's that word?
Gf	*Away*
A	*'Away we go.'*
	'Go! Go! Go!'
	'No! No! No!'
	'Bed (Bath) and //
Gf	That was Bath wasn't it?
A	*'Bath and bed,' Mum said.*
	What's that?
Gf	*Splash*
A	*'Splash in the bath,' said Ned.*
	What's that?
Gf	*Into*
A	*'Into bed, Ned.'*
Gf	That's lovely Alice.
	You read that really well.
	(4 years 5 months)

Alice appeared to be reading in a conventional manner, slowly and deliberately, even correcting the word order. She apparently thought that either she could read the word, in which case she did, or that she didn't recognise it, in which case she asked what it was. She paid close attention to each word, following each with her finger even though she could probably have recited the book through perfectly. It was indisputable that she could read certain words and she had a clear visual memory of them. This was also apparent when she was drawing and writing:

A   Shall I write some words.
Gf   Okay what words did you want to write?
A   *no*
        That says no.
Gf   It does doesn't it?
A   *to*
Gf   What's that one you've done?
A   It's to.
        And there's
          And
Gf   It is and, that's lovely.
A   I'll do
          Alice
        now.
Gf   That's it.
A   And
          CAitlin
Gf   You have done a lot of writing haven't you?

Alice had finished and was selecting another piece of paper to do a drawing. She had written five words accurately, although she used an upper case <A> from her own name quite regularly in other words which required only the lower case. For the moment Alice was reluctant to write words which she could not represent conventionally.

A few days later when I was working on my word processor Alice came into my study and stood watching me for a few moments. Then she indicated the words that she could recognise on the screen.

A There's an 'and'.
Gf It is, what else can you see?
A 'the' (pointing to the word on the screen)
Gf That is 'the'.
A 'to' and 'up'
Gf That's right, I didn't know that you knew 'up'.
A It's the opposite of down.
Gf Mm, up and down.
A They're in my Barney book.
Gf Oh they are aren't they, I remember now.
A Shall I write the words?
Gf Okay, you sit there and write them on one of my sheets of paper.

Alice sat on the floor and wrote a list of six words plus her name: to, And, the, up, no, do, Alice. After she had written her list I asked her about the word 'do', which we hadn't talked about before she started to write.

Gf What's that word?
A That's 'do'.
   You know, like in 'Do you want to be my friend?'
Gf Oh yes, I remember it's 'Do you want to be my friend?' That's lovely Alice.

So although Alice was demonstrating her knowledge of some words and her ability to write them accurately, she was also linking them to previously read stories.

Some books were read with the focus on the story, such as another Hairy Maclary, *Hairy Maclary's Bone* (Dodd, 1984). As Alice got to know the story she contributed large sections of the text whenever it was read, but without appearing to play close attention to each word and concentrating instead on the story line:

A *Hairy Maclary's Bone*
Gf Do you want to read that one again?
A Yes, I do.

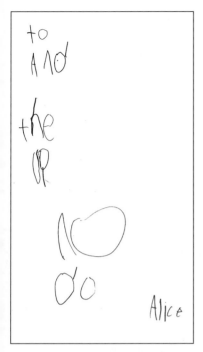

Figure 9: Words Alice could write, to, and , the, up, no, do. 4 years 5 months.

Gf   Okay, come on then.

Down in the town

A   *by the butcher's shop*

sat Hairy Maclary

from Donaldson's Dairy.

(4 years 5 months)

The way that first page was read was typical. An adult would read the first line, or sometimes just part of it, and Alice would provide the rest. On other occasions Alice thought more about letters and words. When she read *Time for bed NED* once more, she miscued the word 'Not' and read 'Ned', perhaps because 'Not' had a capital <N>:

A   *'Ned! Bed, I said.'*

'No. Ned (Not) bed.'

(Looks again at the page)

'No. // Not bed.'

Gf   That's right.

It's Not isn't it.

How did you work that out?

A   I saw the <t> at the end.

(4 years 6 months)

Clearly, then, Alice was looking closely at the word and using the letter ending as well as the initial letter. It might have been her memory that led her to pause when she miscued Not as Ned. Or she might have noted the <t> and recognised the mismatch, as she informed me. Her reflection upon her miscue and prompt self-correction shows how retrospective miscue analysis (RMA) might be used in a simple format with young children (Marek, 1991; Campbell, 1993).

Alice had by now cut up some of the rhymes that she had enjoyed reading, singing and writing so that she had a collection of words which she liked reorganising into the original rhyme or using to create new sentences. She came up with:

Caitlin and Alice go to the zoo.

Alice herself added a few words on small pieces of paper, such as 'no', 'mum', 'dad', 'a' and she requested adults to write a few more for her. 'Went', 'swimming pool' and 'with' became part of her collection. Alice took considerable delight in arranging the small pieces of paper with these words on to create new sentences:

Alice and Caitlin went to the swimming pool.

Next Alice wanted to have 'Once upon a time' written for her, on a single piece of paper:

A   So that I can write a story.

The story she wrote, complete with pictures, was:

Once upon a time mum and Caitlin went to the swimming pool.

Perhaps because her production was derived from playing with the words, she concentrated on the words first and only then produced the pictures to go alongside. More typically young children draw the pictures first, then add the words, and Alice normally did so too. For the moment, however, her collection of words appeared to encourage her to construct a sentence first.

Reading books in the two different ways continued for some weeks. Alice read some with almost total recall of the story line and little apparent attention to the print on the page but others she read more slowly and deliberately, paying attention to the print and often following the words with her finger. She read another of the books by Lynley Dodd *Sniff – Snuff – Snap!* (Dodd, 1995) in 'memory' style, the adult making a small input and Alice a major contribution:

Gm   *Two yellow weaver birds,*
                passing by.
A   *'EEEEEEEE!'*
                squealed the warthog,
                'SNIFF – SNUFF – SNAP!
                He chased them away ...
                BUT
                they both sneaked back.
                Back to the waterhole,
                green and brown
                and slowly,
                the water went down
                and down.

This sequence is pretty well repeated throughout the story as other animals come down to the waterhole and the warthog tries to chase them away. Alice read the familiar section that followed each event. At the end of the story, where the warthog finds an empty waterhole, Alice could read the last two pages.

A   *Back came the warthog,*
                tired and hot,
                for a long,
                cool drink
                at his favourite spot.
                Down past rocks
                and thornbush tree,
                he came to the waterhole
                BUT
                what did he see?
                THICK
                BROWN
                MUD

After Alice knew the story well she took to adding to the story. In the pictures the sky gradually gets blacker, and as the warthog stares at the

THICK BROWN MUD a drop of rain splashes on his back. Based on this information Alice provided her own ending:

A   Drip, drop, drip.
The rain came down
and filled up the waterhole again.
(4 years 7 months)

Alice read the much shorter book, *Paddington at the Seaside* (Bond, 1992c) far more deliberately:

A   *Paddington*
at the
What's that word?
Gm   Well, where is Paddington?
A   The seaside.
Gm   That's right, it says seaside.
A   *seaside*
Paddington is
at the seaside.
He//
Gm   *finds*
A   *finds a//*
Gm   That's a deckchair, like you had on holiday.
A   *deckchair,*
Gm   That's it
He finds a deckchair,
then
A   *then goes for a swim.*
(The picture of Paddington swimming helps her read this page).
(4 years 7 months)

The reading continued like this with Alice reading some of the words, asking about some, and being given others such as 'then' in order to maintain the momentum of her reading.

Figure 10: A story. 4 years 7 months.

At this stage, Alice was also drawing pictures with a name added, writing shopping lists, birthday cards and stories. She also decided to write a book about Alice. On the five pages of the book she wrote:

> I go to the swimming pool.
> I go to the zoo.
> I go to the park.
> I go to bed.
> I go to the shops.

In the safety of this restricted number of words Alice needed only to ask an adult to write 'swimming pool', 'park' and 'shops' for her. She was confident that she could write the rest on her own. Opposite each sentence Alice drew a picture, so her book resembled the many picture books she had experienced.

Alice came to visit clutching a new book, *There's a monster in my house* (Tyler and Hawthorn, 1996). She was excited and wanted to tell me about it and have it read to her:

A	I've got a new book.
Gf	You have, I don't think I know that one.
A	Guess what it's called.
Gf	I don't know.
A	*There's a monster in my house.*
Gf	That sounds good. Are there monsters in it?
A	Not really.
	You read it to me.
Gf	Okay let's read it.
	(Turns to the first page)
	That looks like a monster.
A	But it's not really, look you have to move the flap.
Gf	Oh, I see.
A	*There's a monster in my house*
	It's hungry, fierce and fat!
	Don't be silly Milly
	I think it's only ...
	... cat!

Figure 11: Grandma and grandad. 4 years 8 months.

	See it was only the cat.
Gf	It was, wasn't it?
A	(turns the page)
	Look on every page there's a spider, a mouse and a duck.
Gf	I didn't notice them.
A	You have to look for them 'cos they're hiding.
Gf	They are aren't they?

A   *There's a monster in my house*
        It's hiding in its den.
        Don't be silly Milly
        I think it's only ...
        ... hen!
        (4 years 8 months)

Alice read like this right to the end of the book. So although she had asked me to read it to her, in the event she read it to me – and was almost word perfect. She knew the story and recited it with appropriate intonation. But although her reading was largely a matter of recall, Alice did occasionally use her finger to remind herself where she was in the text, and she did this accurately. It was the rhythm of the story and the repetition of the two sequences which helped Alice to read the complete book with such enjoyment.

Alice still returned regularly to the earlier books which had caught her imagination. She had just got a new kitten so she decided to write a story about it, using a few simple words she knew plus the word kitten. It was fascinating that she integrated the theme from *Time for bed NED* (Zinnemann-Hope, 1986) into her story, which read:

> Alice and her kitten
> They played with a ball.
> Mummy said lunch.
> Alice said no.
> Mummy said yes yes.
> Alice had lunch.

Figure 12: The front cover of Alice's book. 4 years 8 months.

The 'no' and the 'yes yes' are a prominent feature of *Time for bed NED* though the adult-child fight is about going to bed rather than eating lunch. It clearly demonstrates the influence of stories upon children's language and their subsequent writing. Two days later this link was made even more apparent as Alice sat beside me at the computer and typed in the first three words of a story before she got me to complete the typing task following her words:

> Alice and her kitten play with a ball.
> Mummy said, 'No Alice it's time for bed.'
> Alice went to bed.
> (4 years 8 months)

A week or so later it was *Tyrone the horrible* (Wilhelm, 1988) that Alice brought to the house to share with me and her grandmother. For once all I had to do was read the complete text to her and Caitlin. The sisters often looked at books together and sometimes Alice would read the story to Caitlin.

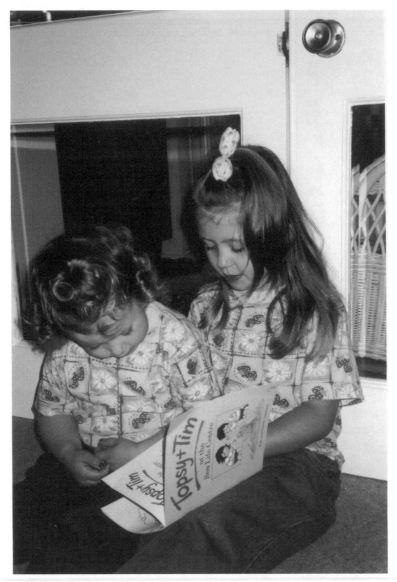

Picture 13: Alice and Caitlin read a Topsy and Tim book. 4 years 8 months.

But there is a lot of print in this book and for the moment Alice was content to listen to the story. She also wanted to recall some of it in writing. Using some key words from the book itself, especially relating to the characters Tyrone and Boland, together with some of the words that she had by now collected, she wrote her story:

> Once upon a time Tyrone
> stamped on Boland's tail.
> He had a fight.
> He burnt himself.
> Tyrone stayed away and Boland
> played happily with his friends.
> (4 years 8 months)

One day when Alice and Caitlin joined us for lunch the conversation suddenly changed direction as Alice asked a literacy based question:

C	I can wink.
Gf	Can you?
C	Look, one eye closed.
Gf	It is a wink, I'll see if I can do one.
C	You did it.
A	How do you write book?
Gm	Book.
	Let me see if I can work it out.
	I wonder what it starts with?
A	/b/
Gm	You're right it's /b/ – book.
	What else do you need?
A	/g/
Gm	Like the /g/.
	I think it's /k/.
A	Mmh. Book.
Gm	So, it goes <b>, <o> <o>, <k>.
Gf	I know another one just like that.
	Look <l>, <o> <o>, <k>.
Gm	And someone in the kitchen – cook.

A   I've got one – took.
Gf   That's right – took. <t>, <o> <o>, <k>.
C   I can wink with my other eye.
Gf   You can can't you.
     (4 years 9 months)

During this exchange Alice demonstrated her ability to recognise the first letter of a word and to hear the rhyme in a group of words and provide an appropriate rhyming word with the same rime element, /ook/. This ability would support her well in her future reading and writing. Meanwhile, Caitlin reminded everyone about what the conversation was about for her: 'I can wink'.

Another literacy exchange was precipitated by the book, *Topsy and Tim at the Sea Life Centre* (Adamson and Adamson, 1997), which I had read to Alice. Alice continued to look through the book and then at the inside cover where the other Topsy and Tim titles were listed:

A   We haven't got that one.
Gf   Which one?
A   Number 8.
Gf   What's number 8?
A   *Topsy and Tim go to the zoo.*
Gf   That's right.
         Topsy and Tim go to the zoo.
     We haven't got that one have we?
     (4 years 9 months)

Alice appeared to have read the eighth title independently, showing her ability to scan through the print and read something without adult support. The 'go to the zoo' phrase contained words she had read, and written, in other contexts. Nevertheless, it was interesting to note her ability to discriminate those words from all the other print and to read that title from among the eighteen titles printed on that page. This was reflected in her ability also to think about letters and words and produce writing. On one sheet of paper she wrote:

yo-yo apple ink dog

and at the bottom of the sheet her name, 'Alice'.

In between these two pieces of writing was a picture and a collection of five letter-like shapes, the fifth being an <e>.

Gf You've written a lot of words.
    What have you got?
A   yo-yo, apple, ink and dog.
    And my name at the bottom.
Gf I can see your name.
    But what's this word?
A   That's how I used to write my name when was I little.
Gf You did didn't you.
    (4 years 10 months)

The surprising aspect of this writing was not the five words, including her own name, that she had written conventionally but that she had also written her name as she 'used to write' it.

Alice was also continuing to write her short stories. Sometimes these were written with me at my computer. On one occasion she typed in very carefully and slowly:

Alice and Caitlin and mummy

but then decided to dictate the rest of the story to me and get me to do the typing for her.

go to the post office.
They post a letter
to auntie Mary.
        Alice Campbell
(4 years 11 months)

Alice was able to tell about her experiences and to see this expressed as print – what Goddard (1974) called a language experience approach Furthermore, the intimate knowledge of this experience and the development of the story into print meant that she could read it with

Picture 14: Alice writing. 4 years 11 months.

confidence to others. These short pieces of writing were sometimes written with a clear audience in mind – she wrote to her mum, dad and Aunt Mary.

Immediately after the Christmas vacation Alice started school. The local school had a policy of encouraging the children to take a book home each day to read with an adult. A few days after starting school, Alice asked if she could read her book to me – one from the Ginn 360 series, *fire!* (Oakley, 1988). The early books in the series have a limited number of words, twelve in this case. Words are repeated with 'can' and 'help' each appearing in the text six times out of the total thirty six words. Punctuation is limited to exclamation and question marks, there are no full stops and sentences do not start with capital letters. By the time Alice read the book to me she had quite successfully mastered the text:

A   *Fire!*
                 look!
                 look! help!
                 can you help?
                 can you //come here?
                 we can help you
                 stop! here is my home
                 can you help?
                 we can help you
                 // come
Gf   That's right, that's come again
A   *come here*
                 here we come
                 we can help
                 look!
                 (4 years 11 months)

Alice showed only the two hesitations – at the word 'come', although she read the final 'come' without hesitation. Otherwise she paid careful attention to each word. She read more slowly than with other books, but that seemed to be linked to her wish to read each word accurately.

After reading the book to me, and then doing so for a second time, she asked if we could read a story from her own book of collected stories, the *Toybox – Bumper Story Book* (BBC, 1996). What she wanted was for me to read a story to her and she occasionally read a few words or commented on the story.

Gf	*William*
A	*and the Dog*
Gf	*One morning, William was feeling bored. He decided to go into the garden to play in the rain. He didn't care how wet he got.*
	'Whee! Puddles are great,' he cried, splashing around.
A	We splash in puddles.
Gf	You do don't you.
C	We both do.
Gf	Yes, I know you do. Ah, but look here.
	William's mum came outside to see what all the noise was.
	(4 years 11 months)

This time Alice had read just three words and made a comment relating the text to her own experience. Caitlin's remark: 'We both do' reflected her inclusion in the group as well as linking to Alice's comment. There is a complete contrast between the two readings that afternoon. In one Alice was the reader; in the other she was more of a listener, although still actively participating.

Alice at 5 years old

By the time she was five Alice was demonstrating her literacy knowledge on a daily basis. For instance:

During shared readings Alice now:
  read parts of books to others,
  frequently gave close attention to the print and read word
  by word,
  read accurately by attending to print and the changing
  position of words, such as 'Mum said' and 'said Ned',
  read stories to others using her knowledge of the story and
  the print on the page,
  continued to enjoy repeat readings of well-loved stories,
  read some of these well-known stories right through, paying
  little attention to the print,
  read separate sentences from texts, including 'Topsy and
  Tim go to the zoo',
  made links to aspects of stories in her play and
  conversations, for instance her reference to 'Koala Lou, I do
  love you',
  created new endings to stories, as in Sniff – Snuff – Snap,
  confidently read the short structured books from school,
  continued to enjoy having new stories read to her.

While writing Alice:
  wrote in a conventional form words recalled from stories
she had read, such as 'owl',

  demonstrated an awareness of letters and sounds in words
  as she talked about and wrote words, for instance 'Kipper',
  wrote the words that she knew in a list from time to time,
  regularly wrote the upper case A in her name in other words
  where a lower case letter was correct,
  wrote her own name and her sister's name, conventionally,
  composed short messages for a particular audience, such as
  mum, dad, Aunt Mary,
  could demonstrate how she used to write when she was
  younger!

When Alice wrote about her own experiences she:
enjoyed sentences that described her experiences,
used those sentences and short stories as part of her own
reading,
used some simple words to create her own short rhymes/
stories,
created a collection of words so she could write stories,
wrote a book about Alice using a limited number of words,
used the words and themes of shared stories to create her
own writing.

Alice's knowledge of letters and sounds was evident, as she:
indicated an interest in rhyming words such as cat, sat,
mat, hat, bat, fat,
demonstrated that she paid close attention to initial letters of
words,
also paid attention to last letters, as when she read self-
corrected 'Ned' to 'not',
talked about the letters in words such as 'book'.

When Alice started school a few days before her fifth birthday she was reading some books with confidence and writing words, sentences and stories. There was much to learn, but there was also much already learned as she continued to share books with adults and engage with print in numerous ways.

Chapter 7
From 5 years

On her fifth birthday Alice received an electronic learning toy, a modified computer (VTECH) with a normal qwerty keyboard and a mouse. Alice had experience of computers at home and at her grandparents' house so she could soon manipulate both. One activity that could be played on the machine required filling in the missing letter for objects displayed on the screen, for instance a picture of a pan was presented together with a box with the letters -an. The task was to type in the missing letter, and the computer indicated whether it was correct. Alice went through the ten words in one of the games and these were her responses:

picture	on screen	Alice's word
pan	-an	pan
ear	ea-	ear
nut	-ut	nut
van	-an	van
hair	ha-r	hayr
man	ma-	man
boy	bo-	boy
key	ke-	key
rug	r-g	rug
ant	an-	ant

(5 years)

Thus she got nine of the ten words and 'hayr' came very close to the letter/sound for 'hair'. Because the words she was responding to did not all tally with those in her visual memory, she had to think of the sounds in the word and select the missing phoneme. As Alice played happily with her computer she displayed her growing knowledge of, and ability to use, phonemes.

Alice was becoming more adventurous with her writing and was not afraid to put on paper whatever she wanted to write. No longer did she feel compelled to ask about the spelling of words, as she had only a few months earlier. She was more confident that her writing could be read by others and that she could work out what letters might be in the words she wanted to write. One afternoon she composed some notes of affection. The first was to her mother:

> I luk (like) mummy and love
> you.

This was followed by:

> I love evebobe (everybody)
> in my fame (family).
> (5 years 1 month)

She had included an <r> in between the first <e> and the <v> of everybody but she then crossed it out. The <b> for <d> was not unusual – sometimes she got the <d> in its correct orientation and sometimes she reversed it. More importantly, her writing contained conventionally composed words and others in her invented, or developmental, spelling (Graves, 1983). These developmental spellings were a further indication of Alice's ability to hear words and recognise which phonemes might need to be represented in print.

Alice was also reading a variety of books on her own and with adults. One day Caitlin visited the library with her grandmother and brought home four books including *Fur* (Mark, 1997). Alice had not seen this book before, and promptly declared that she wanted to read it. Before she began she talked briefly about the title:

Gm   What do you think this book is about?

A   *Fun (Fur)*

Gm   No, that word is like Fun though.

A   /f/ /u/ /r/

Gm   What is on the cat?

A   Hair.

Gm   What do we call cat's hair?

A   Fur

          This (Thin) Kitten (Kitty) grew fat.

          /s/ /h/ /e/

Gm   /sh/

A   *She made a nice (nest) in my hat,*

Gm   What do you think this might be?

A   Nice.

Gm   It's like nice, but what do birds build in a tree?

A   nest

Gm   Yes, a nest

          another

A   *another in the kitten (kitchen) cupboard*

Gm   Yes

          another in the kitchen cupboard

A   *and a //*

Gm   *third*

A   *third on Mum's skirt.*

          But she liked the hat nice-nest best.

Gm   Yes

          the hat nest best.

A   *All night she played (purred)*

Gm   *purred*

A   *and now my hat is full of fur.*

          Kittens.

        (5 years 1 month)

The way that Alice read this text that was new to her demonstrated how far she had come as a reader. She had made just five substitutions:

(spoken word)	(text word)
this	thin
kitten	kitty
nice	nest
kitten	kitchen
played	purred

The list shows the close resemblance between the text and Alice's substitute. Miscue analysis (Goodman, Watson and Burke, 1987; Campbell, 1993) would note that the spoken word and text word were similar in their graphophonic or letter/sound features.

It was not just the graphophonic features that Alice appeared to be using. Her first miscue was 'This' (Thin) – a miscue which retained the sentence structure and much of the text's meaning. Furthermore Alice's word was typically used at the start of a sentence in many of the books she read. She was using her background knowledge of how books work, as well as cues from the specific text, as she read.

The next substitution, 'kitten' (kitty) is a close approximation and a reasonable deduction from the illustration. Next, Alice tried to sound out the word 'she', but her grandmother provided the /sh/ sound for her. The third substitution was 'nice' (nest), which leads to a breakdown in meaning and sentence structure. There was then a discussion about the word, which guided Alice to an awareness that the text word was 'nest'. The fourth substitution 'kitten' (kitchen) – is extremely close in graphophonic features, only a <t> for a <ch>. And although the cupboard is in the kitchen the meaning of the story is not disrupted by reading 'kitten'.

As Alice hesitated at 'third', her grandmother provided the word to help her keep going. Then Alice again read 'nice' (nest) but this time self-corrected her miscue. Her final miscue was reading 'played' for 'purred'. and this changes the meaning of the sentence, although Alice does retain the sentence structure by providing a verb, as required. Again these words are very similar in their graphophonic features.

Alice's reading of the story was not totally unaided. But although her grandmother supported her, Alice was largely in control and she was reading a text which she had not previously met. Clearly she could now read simple stories conventionally and also, as the five substitutions showed, she was using a well developed knowledge of letters, sounds, sentences and meaning in her reading.

After Alice read the story she went out into the garden to play with her new skipping rope. She was beginning to acquire the skill of skipping, the current school playground activity which she appeared determined to perfect. As she skipped she provided a retelling of the story:

Gm   Did you like that story?
A   Yes.
Gm   And what was the story about?
A   It was about a thin cat that got fat.
Gm   Why did it get fat?
A   'cos it was going to have babies.
Gm   Mmh it was. So what did the cat do?
A   It made a nest in the hat, then in the kitchen
          cupboard, then on Mum's skirt. Then she had her kittens.
Gm   Where did she have her kittens?
A   In the hat because she liked it best.

This was about ten minutes after the single reading of *Fur*. Obviously she was able to read the story with some accuracy and had also absorbed the story line. Alice's retelling provided the story line and some of the details, such as her comments about a 'nest' in the hat, and in the 'kitchen' cupboard. Although she had miscued these words she used them correctly when retelling the story.

As Alice's confidence in reading grew, so did her confidence in writing. In quick succession, one weekend morning, she produced three pieces of writing. The first was a book; actually a piece of A4 paper folded in half to create four sides. The front page contained a picture and the title of the story:

(written text)	(intended text)
Alice's dog	Alice's dog

On the middle two pages Alice wrote her story:

Alice's	Alice's
mum sed	mum said
we uur	we are
geting	getting
a dog	a dog
ep ep	hip hip
hray	hooray
sed	said
Alice	Alice

Alice was now willing to be a risk-taker and write any word, using her knowledge of sounds to construct it. Alice could write 'bed' accurately, so 'sed' was perfectly logical. Her other developmental spellings were close approximations to the sounds of the words. That a double consonant is required before the -ing ending in certain verbs such as get, would have to be learnt in due course.

Alice also used some punctuation, placing an apostrophe appropriately in 'Alice's'. This suggests that not only was Alice learning about letters and sounds and the construction of words, but she was also beginning to recognise other features of written language. It would be more typical for her to have used full stops, exclamation and question marks, and quotation marks first (Hall and Robinson, 1996). By beginning with the possessive apostrophe, Alice reminds us that each child will make their own journey in understanding the complexities of print.

Underneath the title 'Alice's dog' on her front cover Alice drew a picture of the dog's head with a speech bubble saying 'wuf' (woof) – further evidence of Alice's awareness of sounds and how they might be represented in print. It also showed that she had noted another convention of print in the depiction of speech.

Figure 13: Alice's dog. 5 years 1 month.

The next book Alice wrote was non-fiction. The writing on the front cover, above a picture of a ladybird, indicated this:

ifmasn	information
book	book

The two inside pages contained information about snails and ladybirds:

sayl	snail
sayls hav	snails have
the shl on is dak	the shell on its back
ldybed	ladybird
ldybed	ladybird
hv	have
wig	wings

In each of the unconventional spellings Alice's use of the sound system can be detected. In particular, 'ifmasn' for 'information' demonstrated her willingness to attempt long and quite complex words. The other spellings of 'dak' for 'back' and 'ldybed' for 'ladybird' were less easy to decipher, partly because Alice had developed a strategy of putting a loop or circle on each side of the vertical line. The reader was left to interpret the letter as either a <b> or a <d>. For the moment that served to solve Alice's problem of how to write these letters.

Finally, Alice produced a picture of an elephant. She created a colour-by-numbers activity, dividing the shape of the elephant into smaller sections and then putting in a colour guide down the side of the paper, so emulating an activity that Alice had seen being completed by older children at school and relating also to a story she liked about *Elmer the Patchwork Elephant* (McKee, 1989). Alice wrote a colour guide for each of the sections:

1 yelo	yellow
2 grin	green
3 dak (or bak)	black

Figure 14: Information book. 5 years 1 month.

4 red	red
5 pupl	purple

Alice then followed her own guide and coloured the elephant to look like Elmer. Once again each of Alice's words are very close approximations of the sound of the words – especially 'yelo'.

At school Alice was reading books with a controlled vocabulary which she brought home and so read both at school and at home; and the adults at school and at home filled in a notebook which served as a reading record so that Alice's reading could be monitored. One day Alice wanted to read me her school book *I can hide* (Ginn New Reading Level 2, 1993):

A   *I will hide.*
               Can you look
               for me, Liz?
               Yes, Ben.
               You go and hide.
               We will look for-look for you.
               Can Digger help us
               look for you?
               Yes, Digger you-can help you.
               Can I hide in there (here)
        Is it there?
Gf   Have a good look, what do you think?
A   *here*
Gf   That's it.
A   *Can I hide in here, Dad?*
               No, Ben.
               You can't hide in here.
               Can-Can I hide in this?
               No, I can't.
               I-Can I hide in here?
               No, Ben.
               You can't hide in here.
               Come (Out) //

Gf   Read the rest and we'll come back to that word.

A   No, you have to try and get that word first.

      //

Gf   */Ou/*

A   *Out you go.*

      I can hide up here.

      Help us look for Ben, Digger.

      Here we come, Ben.

      Look.

      Ben is up here.

      I can't //

      Instead of out it's

      /g/ /e/ /t/ get down!

      Help me, Liz.

      We will help you, Ben.

      We will get you down.

      (5 years 1 month)

Alice read the text very deliberately, obviously paying very close attention to each word. She was very accurate. There were a number of repetitions of a word or words, such as 'look for' and 'Can', which may have been a way of confirming what she was reading or considering the word to be read next. Alice also self-corrected her reading with 'you-can' and later in the text 'I-can'. Such self-corrections, Clay (1972) argued, are a useful sign that the young reader is checking her reading as she proceeds; then returning to self-correct where the information provided by the letters, sounds, sentence structure and meaning suggest something else.

Alice clearly verbalised one of her self-corrections when she met the text word 'get'. First, she indicated that 'instead of out it's', comparing 'out', which she read earlier, with the text's 'get'. The words have some graphic similarity. Immediately she decided that 'out' was not right, she sounded out each of the word's phonemes /g/ /e/ /t/. and then accurately read 'get' and proceed to the end of the book.

Alice had also produced two substitutions: 'there' for 'here' and 'come' for 'out' and her subsequent comments and questions were interesting. With the first, Alice recognised that her spoken word was not a perfect match for the text word so she simply asked whether it was 'there'. Her question suggests that she was already thinking it might be wrong and when directed to look at the word again she produced an accurate reading of 'here'. She then read the complete sentence again; perhaps she felt she had to remind herself of the text after the interruption.

The substitution of 'Come' for 'Out' created a greater problem. After reading 'Come', Alice hesitated, which might mean that she had been reconsidering her spoken word but she rejected my suggestion to read on before trying the word again in the belief that you had to get each word right before carrying on reading. My assistance with the initial sound helped Alice to read 'Out' and carry on.

In contrast to such deliberate reading of school books Alice still greatly enjoyed sharing books with the adult doing most of the reading. As Alice herself said after reading her school book: 'Soon I'll be able to read real books'. For the moment Alice accepted having what she called real books read to her. In quick succession she requested the ever popular *Mr Gumpy's Outing* (Burningham, 1970) and then a more recent book which she and Caitlin both loved, *The Last Noo-Noo* (Murphy, 1995).

As Alice continued to write she paid increasing attention to punctuation. After a car journey and a visit to a local forest, Alice wrote inside a card:

> to Grandad R.
> thank you for.
> the Gane (journey) in the.
> car.
>
> Love from.
> Alice.
> (5 years 2 months)

Figure 15: A card for grandad. 5 years 2 months.

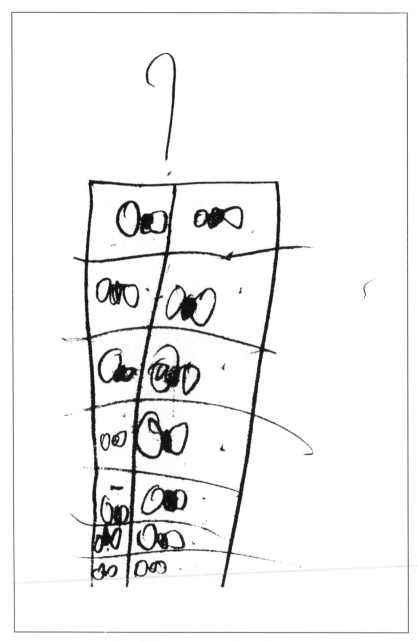

Figure 16: A question mark. 5 years 2 months.

When I asked her about the dots at the end of each line she indicated:

A   My teacher said you have to put a full stop at the end of
      each sentence.

For the moment Alice was linking the concept of a sentence to the graphic feature of a line (see Hall and Robinson, 1996) but she was considering a range of punctuation signs. On a birthday card to her great-grandmother, she drew a picture of a box on the front with a question mark above it because 'You have to work out what's inside'. Punctuation had become another part of the writing process for Alice.

Although the intention of this book had been to trace Alice's progress as a reader before she began school, the significant developments that took place a few months either side of her fifth birthday warranted recording observations for a few months after she started school. Now five years and two months old, Alice had demonstrated over the space of a couple of weeks and with four different literacy activities just what she had achieved. First, her careful reading of a simple story book, *Fur* (Mark, 1997), which she read on seeing it for the first time, demonstrated her progress as a reader. Her subsequent retelling indicated how she was able to comprehend a text she was reading for the first time. Second, the two stories she wrote and her colouring task provided evidence of a command of language, letters and sounds which enabled her to write whatever she wanted. That knowledge would serve her well whenever she was confronted with unknown words in her reading. Furthermore, she was now paying attention to the conventions of punctuation. Third, there was Alice's largely accurate reading of a controlled vocabulary school book in which she showed that not only was she reading but that she was also reflecting on her own reading and self-correcting where the graphophonic, syntactic and semantic information called for it. Fourth, Alice still enjoyed sharing books with an adult and having stories read to and with her, and this pleasure and love of books suggested that not only would Alice become a independent reader but that she would retain the motivation to read.

Chapter 8
Learning from Alice

The significant adults in her life much enjoyed reading with Alice. It was a time when a story was shared and relationships were nurtured and Alice learned a great deal and her literacy developed. However, the adults were in turn also learning from Alice about the activities and experiences which were encouraging Alice towards literacy.

Six key activities in particular appeared to contribute substantially to Alice's literacy development: the numerous readings and rereading of books; the opportunities for writing, writing her own name; looking at letters; and the songs, nursery rhymes and rhyming books which supported Alice's literacy development. Each of these activities is now considered.

Story reading

Throughout the first five years of her life Alice had books read to and with her regularly and frequently. The 68 children's books noted in the references here are a record merely of those Alice shared when she was observed each month. She actually shared many more books than this over the years at home and with her grandparents and friends, and when she went to the library. Alice probably had hundreds of different books read to her in her first five years.

The importance of story readings has long been recognised: Jim Trelease (1989) and Margaret Meek (1990) are among the many who have chronicled the benefits children gain from being read to at home. The benefits for Alice were evident from a very early stage, for instance her delight in sharing *Spot's first words* when she was 7 months. And her pleasure sustained her interest in being read stories.

For the early readings a variety of approaches were adopted. Sometimes the book was simply read to her but more usually it was like a conversation, as the adult and Alice together considered the objects and characters in the illustrations. When reading *Forest Friends* (1 year 9 months) for instance, the decision as to how the reading proceeded was determined by Alice and the questions she asked. At other times the adult told the story rather than reading it, even though the book – such as *Bambi* (1 year 7 months) – was being used as the guide to the telling. In all these circumstances Alice demonstrated her real involvement and interest in the books.

This was extended once she could provide some of the reading herself. The first time was apparently when reading *Oh Dear!* (1 year 11 months), where she provided the key phrase at the appropriate times. And as we saw, she carried that phrase over into her oral language and often used it during play and contact with her parents. Within a few months Alice was providing the words for large sections of a story (*Tuffy the Jeep*, 2 years 4 months) and for even longer texts (*Good-Night Owl*, 2 years 9 months), especially where the rhythm and the repetition of phrases helped her to memorise the words of the book. As she approached the age of three, Alice also demonstrated other reading behaviour, reading books to her younger sister, following a few words with her finger under the print, and sitting by herself reading a book out loud.

The reading of books or part of books became still more firmly established during the next year (*The Very Hungry Caterpillar*, 3 years 5 months). Memorisation of books was an important part of Alice's progress as a reader. First it enabled her to perform as a reader and show that she was in control of the text. Then it lead gradually to connecting such memorised readings with recognising certain words in the text. In part she achieved this by asking questions about words. Her question at 3 years 9 months 'Why has egg got an <s>?', while looking at the word 'eggs' was indicative of her close attention to words.

Alice eventually brought together her recall of text and her close attention to print. When she read *Time for bed Ned* (4 years 5 months), for instance, Alice read deliberately, slowly and clearly paying attention to each word – even though she knew the book in its entirety and could recite it from memory. She now wanted to match that knowledge of the book with each word of the text.

By this stage Alice was prepared to read simple picture books that were new to her. Just after her fifth birthday (5 years 1 month), she confidently approached the book *Fur* even though she had not seen it before. Her reading of the forty one words in the book with only five miscues, proclaimed Alice as a reader and it also showed how it was she who was often now the reader. Reading with Alice had increasingly become reading by Alice.

The number of different books which were read to Alice supported her literacy development. Her involvement in the story readings, her use of language from the books at other times, her gradually increasing contributions to the readings and eventually her own individual reading of books, testified to that development. And throughout, there was Alice's continual enjoyment of the books and her pleasure in sharing them with a significant adult.

The success of story readings with Alice has implications for the extent to which story reading features in nursery, reception, or preschool classrooms. Of course, early years teachers read stories to young children. But, are these readings as regular and frequent as they need to be? Are children in their first classroom having hundreds of books read to them over a year? Are the children in early years classrooms having the same benefits from story readings as Alice and children like her? These are important questions for those who work with young children.

Many early years teachers make use of big books in a shared book experience so that the children can all see the print (Holdaway, 1979). But these story readings and the continuing involvement with the stories may not be repeated often enough to be optimally useful. The restrictions that teachers feel the national curriculum imposes on them may limit the number of story readings they give young children. Observations from my study, which builds upon earlier longitudinal projects such as reported by Wells (1986) should support teachers in arguing for the positive influence of story readings on children's literacy development.

Rereading

Alice derived pleasure and learning from story readings. Highly significant, however, was the frequent repetition. Not only did Alice have hundreds of stories read to her but most were read many times over. These repeat readings were already a feature during Alice's first year, elicited from her parents and grandparents by her evident delight each time a particular book was shared with her. Alice's hearty laughter as she shared repeatedly *Spot's first words* (7 months) with her mother one lunchtime, is a lasting memory for all who witnessed the event.

It was these repeat readings that led to Alice quickly memorising part of the story and then contributing it to the reading. Her contribution of 'Oh dear!' in the story of that name occurred before she turned 2 (1 year 11 months). Such learning was certainly aided by the rhythm and the recurring phrases or sentences in many of the books. Such books support the children's reading because they are enjoyable and because the child can soon participate.

It was soon clear that Alice was asking to have stories repeated. At 2 years 5 months, she said 'Read it again.' immediately after *Baby Owl* was read to her, and this became a recurring request – in the very same words that Payton (1984) had noted in the study of her daughter. Children like to have stories repeated so that they can develop knowledge and ownership of the story and begin to take part in the reading themselves.

Complying with requests to read the book again can mean that the adult has to read a book as many as eight times at one sitting, as happened with *Jasper's Jungle Journey* (3 years) borrowed from the library.

Successive rereadings enabled Alice to memorise almost entirely, and therefore control, books such as *Good-Night Owl* (3 years).

Alice continued to request repeat readings of favourite books right through the study and she began to use her knowledge of the books to begin reading them carefully for herself and also for her own writing. We saw how she read *Time for bed Ned* (4 years 5 months) word by word relying on her memory of the story to connect each word in the text. Thus did she read in a conventional sense of paying attention to the print. When she wrote 'do', she explained: 'That's do. You know, like in *Do you want to be my friend?*' (4 years 5 months).

So there are good reasons why children want to have stories they like read repeatedly. Some books were probably read to Alice more than ten times in one day, because she wanted to hear the story again and again. This rereading is desired because of the sheer delight in the text, but it also enables her to know the book and so acquire ownership of the words. Once children know the text they too can behave like a reader with a book. And with each of the readings the young child learns more about books, print, words, letters, links with the illustrations, authorship and so on.

The experience of Alice, and children like her, raises questions about how many books are read repeatedly in pre-school settings. Frequent rereadings certainly help children to gain control of text. Yet early years teachers are less likely to reread stories repeatedly and might need to reconsider their practice.

Opportunities for writing

This book has followed Alice's relationship with story books during her first five years and considered some of the key features related to story readings. Other studies (e.g. Bissex, 1980) have focused on writing development and the present study is concerned mainly with reading. It nevertheless indicates how Alice developed as a writer during her first five years, because her progress in reading and writing were interwoven.

Before Alice was two she was expressing an interest in writing by asking for a 'pen' (1 year 11 months) and producing circular patterns on paper. By the time she was 2 years 4 months it was possible to distinguish between the pictures she drew and her writing of words. A picture, typically of some named person, would consist of a circle with some representation of eyes, nose and mouth, while her writing was generally a sequence of wavy horizontal lines. She was thus demonstrating an important discrimination between pictures and writing. Two months later (2 years 6 months) Alice was producing separate squiggles rather than a horizontal line and naming these squiggles with a letter of the alphabet. These squiggles or pseudoletters could not be recognised as letters but just before her third birthday (2 years 11 months) Alice wrote 'too' as a collection of letters rather than as a word, and announced that it was a '<t> and two <o>s'.

As Alice developed her understanding of writing she used a number of different strategies. She represented syllables on the page with a mark for each syllable that she heard (3 years 3 months). She used her own forename as a means of learning how to represent words (see below). Then for a while she wanted to write only what was accurate, so she would ask an adult questions such as 'How do you write whale?' when she wanted to caption her drawings (3 years 10 months). Later she acquired a collection of accurately written words on small pieces of paper, which she arranged and rearranged into sentences and short stories (4 years 6 months). These words such as 'mum', 'dad', 'and', 'go', 'went', 'zoo', 'to', 'the', 'Caitlin', became part of her visual memory of words and she could then write them whenever she wanted.

At much the same stage, Alice wrote using her own invented or developmental spellings such as 'wll' for 'wall' (3 years 11 months). Her willingness to write without asking an adult for a spelling became pronounced by her fifth birthday. By then she felt able to write whatever she wanted to write, knowing that she could use the sounds of the words to say what she wanted in print without receiving any direct instruction she felt confident that she could say a word, recognise the sounds in it, and then represent those sounds in print, although this did not always lead to an accurate and conventional writing.

The books that she constructed: 'Alice's dog' and the 'ifmasn book' (5 years 1 month), were indicative of her new-found confidence as an independent writer and a risk-taker. Writing 'ifmasn' for 'information' is one example of Alice's careful attempts to represent in writing the sounds she recognised in a word. These two books also indicated that the adults in her home environment as well as her teachers at school were supporting Alice in her endeavours as a risk-taker.

Alice's writing and reading supported each other and developed hand in hand. Sometimes the link between her writing and reading was explicit, for instance, at 4 she wrote the word 'owl', saying that it was like – 'and owl tried to sleep' – an explicit reference to *Good-Night Owl!* Along with another much-read book, *Baby Owl,* it encouraged Alice to think about owls and to recognise the word 'owl'. As she wrote it, she made it part of her written and reading vocabulary. Alice's reading supported her writing and her writing added to her development as a reader.

Writing her own name

It is often the child's forename which becomes the first word to be explored. Indeed Davies (1988) suggested that children's involvement with writing their forenames provides a bridge into literacy. Alice demonstrated her interest in writing her forename at 2 years 6 months when she said she was 'writing Alice'. At the time her writing contained three pseudoletters, two of which were like an <l> with a vertical line and the third like a <v> or <u>.

By the time she turned three Alice would often produce a piece of writing consisting only of a capital <A>. But very quickly that developed so that by age 3 years 3 months she was regularly writing her name on her pictures. The representation of her name would consistently start with a capital <A> and have five letters. The <l> and <i> would follow the <A> – although not always in that order – and the last two letters would have some form of circular feature.

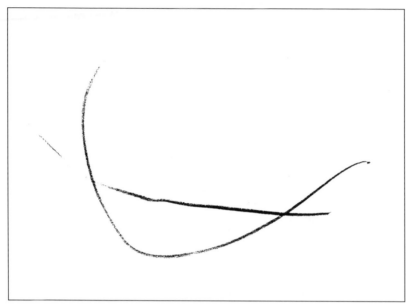

Figure 17: A big A. 3 years.

The daily and frequent attempts at writing her name and her interest in representing it meant that by the time Alice was 3 years 6 months she consistently produced an accurate writing of 'Alice'. Writing her own name was an important achievement for Alice in its own right. However, it also added to her literacy learning because she now had a model of a word. She knew that a word is written separate from other words, that it consists of specific letters, and that the letter sequence is important – all useful knowledge for her writing.

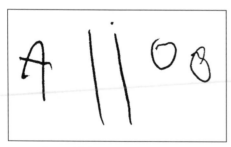

Figure 18: Alice. 3 years 3 months.

Given the importance to her of the word 'Alice' it was no surprise that she wrote 'CAitlin' and 'And' (4 years 5 months) for some months before beginning to use the lower case <a> when appropriate.

Figure 19: Alice and a lion with a mane. 3 years 6 months.

Interestingly, Alice herself reflected on her progress in writing her own name. At 4 years 10 months, she wrote a number of words, drew a picture and added her name. Then on the same sheet she also wrote four pseudoletters and a fifth letter <e> and described this as 'How I used to write my name when I was little'. This shows the literacy learning that Alice had derived from her engagement with her forename.

Looking at letters

Although Alice did not receive any direct instruction about letters and letter sounds, they were discussed, for instance in connection with her large alphabet chart. Her parents would play games with her, using the poster, on the lines of: '<T> is for?'. By 1 year 8 months, Alice was responding to such questions with actions that indicated that she could link the letter names to the objects pictured in her poster. Such games also meant that Alice was developing an awareness of letter shapes, and by the time she was 2, she occasionally demonstrated such recognition. For instance, on receiving a birthday card, she said '<p>' while pointing to this letter in her surname.

Figure 20: How I used to write my name. 4 years 10 months.

For a short time at age 2 years 6 months Alice would ask for a sweet by requesting an '<o>', and later that year she wrote 'too' and described this as: a '<t> and two '<o>s' (2 years 11 months). She also talked about some of the letters on the title page of *Good-Night Owl*, intrigued that 'Owl's sitting in an <o>' (3 years). Her interest in writing her forename meant that by age 3 years 6 months she was able to write the letters accurately and in the correct sequence. And since her requests of 'how do you write ....' typically elicited the letters from an adult (3 years 9 months) she was able to recognise and write each of the letters in the alphabet – although sometimes confusing the orientation, particularly <d> and <b>.

Alice's knowledge of letter shapes and letter names provided a basis for producing her own writing. This required her to give close attention to the sounds of the letters too. While writing 'ovmuA' for 'Kipper' (4 years) she said 'I need a <p> for Kipper', possibly recognising that her word did not look right rather than that the /p/ was missing from her word. Her writing of 'ouvHit' for 'Ruby' similarly led her to ask: 'Where's the <b>?'.

We noted Alice's close attention to letters and letter sounds when she self-corrected a reading miscue (4 years 6 months), while reading *Time for bed Ned*, from 'Ned' to 'Not'. When asked how she worked out that it was 'Not', she replied: 'I saw the <t> at the end'. This is even more obvious when Alice discussed the spelling of the word 'book' (4 years 9 months). When two other words were suggested – look and cook – she replied: 'I've got one – took', showing her awareness of the rime in these words and her ability to cite another word ending with the same sound. The game on her modified computer that required inserting a missing letter – <p> into 'an' – also encouraged Alice to think about letters and letter sounds (5 years).

Alice's willingness to write independently with invented or developmental spellings provided continual involvement with letters and letter sounds. Her little note of affection 'I love evebobe in my fame' (5 years 1 month) indicated her ability to detect the sounds in words and to represent these logically in a written format, while her four conventionally written words showed that she could accurately write the words with which she was familiar.

We can see from Alice's writing how she learned about letters and letter sounds through reading and writing. As Goswami and Bryant (1990) noted, children's 'progress in learning to read (or to read an alphabetic script at any rate) is probably the most important cause of awareness of phonemes' (p 26). The shared story readings, the repeat readings, the opportunities for writing and the games and discussions about the alphabet all ensured that Alice would learn about letters and letter sounds, and would do so naturally without any direct teaching.

Songs, nursery rhymes and rhyming books

As well as having hundreds of books read and reread to her, Alice also heard many songs and nursery rhymes, and eventually joined in their singing. Especially during her first year, songs, rhymes and finger games were a regular feature of her day. As early as 3 months, Alice was playing a small part in some of the songs, for instance, as she anticipated the ending of the adapted Tigger song when her parents would blow air on to her cheek. Like stories, songs were repeated time and time again.

Although her parents hadn't deliberately planned to present her with rhyming words at 6 months, the constant repetition of 'See-saw Marjorie Daw' and the rhymes in many of the finger games such as 'Teddy Bear' (7 months) that adults played with her contributed in due course to Alice's reading development. In the words of Margaret Meek (1990) 'Please teach nursery rhymes, and the phonology will come unnoticed with fun.' (p151). Meek pointed out that nursery rhymes are taught not as a preventative to later reading difficulties but because they are enjoyable, have memorable words and are a rich popular culture.

Alice had great fun playing games such as 'Ring a ring of roses' (1 year 3 months), joining in with others and linking to actions. At the same time she would have been assimilating the rhymes of roses/posies, along with rhymes in some of the books she enjoyed. In *Here's a Happy Pig* (1 year 6 months) the rhyme:

One! Two! Three!
Wiggle and See!

amused Alice over and over for some months. She contributed a few words to books such as *Nursery Rhymes – 1* (2 years) and by 3 years 1 month could recite rhymes such as 'Humpty Dumpty' and 'Hey diddle diddle, the cat and the fiddle,' to her younger sister Caitlin.

There were also the more extended rhymes in the Dr Seuss books, for instance *Green Eggs and Ham* (3 years 8 months) provided sixty two pages of rhyming – which she asked to hear over and over again. She made her understanding of rhymes evident when she said: 'The cat sat on the bricks not on a mat' while listening to *It's My Birthday* (4 years 2 months) went on: 'cat, sat, mat, hat,' and later 'and bat and fat.' Another book with strong rhyming features, *Hairy Maclary from Donaldson's Dairy* (4 years 4 months) remained a firm favourite for many months and the words:

Muffin McLay
like a bundle of hay,
Bottomley Potts
covered in spots,

often cropped up in Alice's and Caitlin's conversations. Alice's incidental learning about rhyming words and her thinking about them and the letters in them came to help her with her writing and reading.

There were a number of other features in Alice's literacy learning that were noted only incidentally. These concerned the role of environmental print, TV print, and the appearance of punctuation. But what underpinned Alice's literacy development most of all were the availability of resources that appealed to her and the supportive adults in her environment.

Environmental print

Naturally Alice saw the significant adults in her life reading newspapers as well as other printed material. As early as 2 years 1 month she emulated that model of literacy use as she picked up a Weekend Magazine from a national newspaper, placed it on the floor in front of her and announced 'Reading'. She also indicated that there were three '<e>s' in the first word of Weekend. On a visit to a supermarket five months later Alice collected the custard powder from the variety of products on display. Whether it was the shape, colours, logo or writing which helped her to identify it, she was involved in a meaningful activity where the print of her environment supported her developing literacy.

At the same age Alice recognised a McDonald's outside her usual environment – probably because of the 'M' logo, or the colours – and also a 'Sainsbury's' supermarket truck, again probably because of the colours, logo and words. At 2 years 10 months, she recognised and named TOYS 'R' US when she saw it out of context and written in blue on a yellow background rather than in its usual multicolours – another illustration of the value of talking with young children about the print in their environment so that they can look at it and read.

Conversations about environmental print became progressively more detailed. When she was 3 years 6 months she noticed the labels on two jars on the table at home and asked about one: 'Does that say Honey?', then observed that 'Pooh likes honey.' Then she asked other questions about the words on the labels and was delighted to find a second example of the words: 'Sainsbury's' and 'jam' on the labels. So Alice used the print in her environment and learned about letters and words in the process.

TV print

Alice liked watching television and learned a good deal, especially, perhaps, from the nature programmes, which brought many different environments into her home and introduced her to a wide variety of animals, some of which she was meeting in books too.

At 2 years 3 months Alice was intrigued with a nature programme on giraffes and watched it to the end. The moment that the first of the closing captions appeared on the screen, she waved and said, 'Bye-bye giraffes'. Her reaction indicated that she was discriminating between pictures and writing, and also that she had already understood a convention of TV whereby the credits – in writing – typically signal the end of the programme.

Alice may also have known about the captions at the start of a programme, but the first time she commented on them was some months later (2 years 11 months). She was watching the start of a video about dolphins and immediately the first caption appeared, Alice asked: 'What's that?' Once she was told what that title read she asked about the next caption: 'What's that now?'. There then followed a brief conversation about dolphins and dugongs before the narrator's name appeared on the screen, and she asked: 'What are those letters?'.

Although this study notes only these two examples, they do demonstrate that Alice looked carefully at the print as well as the pictures on the screen. This confirms that children learn about print from TV – most of all, suggested Torrey (1969), through listening to and looking at the print associated with commercials. In Alice's case her attention to the print on TV added to her literacy learning.

Punctuation

Because this record of literacy development relates to the first five years there are only a few notes about Alice's attention to punctuation. Much of her development in this area was likely to occur as understanding of print became more firmly established (Hall and Robinson, !996). However, when she was 3 years old she did note an exclamation mark while sharing the book, Good-Night Owl! , linking the exclamation mark with a letter <i> and remarking that: 'That one is upside down'.

Although Alice probably continued to look at punctuation marks as she had stories read to her, it was only after her fifth birthday that she started to use any in her own writing, – firstly, the possessive apostrophe in her little book called 'Alice's dog' (5 years 1 month). Then she started to use full stops – first, at the end of each line rather than at the end of a sentence (5 years 2 months). At the same age she used a question mark appropriately in a drawing, indicating that she was aware of its purpose even though she was not incorporating it in her writing. So we can assume that in addition to thinking about the message, the spellings and handwriting of the letters, Alice was now also thinking about using punctuation marks.

Available resources

Alice was fortunate in that she had numerous resources which supported her literacy learning, most importantly perhaps the collections of books she had in her own and her grandparents' homes. When only 11 months old Alice would often crawl to her book collection, select a book, place it on the floor in front of her and look at the pictures in it. For the next four years, Alice continued to choose and look through her books on a frequent and regular basis. She also often selected a book and then asked an adult to read it to her. Alice could also regularly choose books from the local library. Together with her own stocks of books the library visits meant that Alice had engaged with hundreds of books by the time she was five.

Most were story books but she did have some experience of other kinds of books. At 3 years 6 months, she described a gazetteer of maps as 'It's a which way you're going book'. And there were other resources which Alice used to develop her literacy understanding, such as the alphabet poster in her bedroom, newspapers, the print on the TV, various environmental print, and having pencils, crayons and paper to support her interest in drawing and writing.

Alice also became familiar with the computer. At 2 years 6 months she sat and tapped the keyboard while calling out letters – although not the letters she was tapping. By 3 years 10 months she could type a few familiar words onto the screen and took pleasure in printing out the list of words. And because it was her own list she could recognise and remember the words on it. Alice also played a missing letter game on the modified computer she received as a fifth birthday present. Mostly Alice spent her time on computers playing games but she also engaged in activities that were clearly to do with literacy.

Supportive adults

Alice was reading and writing with some confidence by the time she was five years of age, although she had not received any direct literacy teaching. But she had supportive adults who responded to her questions and needs and had frequent literacy interactions with her. Very early on, her mother was singing rhymes to Alice and getting Alice to join in, albeit with non-verbal responses (3 months). Alice was also having conversations with adults around a book. Her father talked about the pictures in a book (4 months), asking Alice about the pictures and providing the answers.

The talking about books and the reading of them by significant adults became a dominant feature of Alice's involvement with literacy. The adults readings those stories encouraged Alice to join in the reading. So by the time she was 1 year 11 months she was encouraged to offer the last line of 'Oh Dear!' in the book so titled. With adult support, her contributions had grown substantially by the time Alice was 3 years old and there were books which she could read almost completely from memory.

Alice's parents and grandparents talked to her about signs and other print in the environment, TV print and the use of the computer, so that all became part of her involvement with print. She benefited from such interactions and from having adults who read to her, talked with her and answered her questions (Clark, 1976).

Later, as Alice began to write extensively, she was aided by adults who encouraged her to take chances as she wrote. The two books that she wrote when she was 5 years 1 month indicated that the adults in her home environment as well as her teachers at school were supporting Alice in her endeavours as a risk-taker. By taking chances she was encouraged to think about the sounds in words and this enabled Alice to produce her developmental spellings with confidence.

Alice's literacy development was facilitated by the significant adults in her life and she in turn began to be a facilitator for her younger sister's literacy development. Alice recited rhymes to Caitlin (3 years 1 month), read books to her (4 years 1 month) and talked about words and letters with her (4 years 9 months). All this helped Caitlin towards literacy, while also extending Alice's own literacy learning. Perhaps most interestingly it indicated that Alice had absorbed the key role of the supportive adult in guiding young children's literacy – a role she repeated with her baby brother Dylan.

Alice supported Caitlin and Dylan but we had all been learning from Alice during her first five years of involvement with literacy. Alice had confirmed the enjoyment and the depth of learning that can take place as stories are read, and she revealed to us a good deal about other key features of literacy learning in the early years. Thank you Alice.

Chapter 9

Literacy learning in early years settings

This book has explored Alice's literacy learning during her first five years at home but it has important messages for those who work with children in early years settings, some of which were signalled in the last chapter. This chapter considers the literacy learning that might be provided for children in early years settings. There is currently renewed emphasis on literacy learning in the early years, as evidenced by *Nursery Education: Desirable Outcomes for Children's Learning* (SCAA, 1996), the use of baseline assessments (SCAA, 1997), and *The National Literacy Strategy* (DfEE, 1998). Such emphasis upon literacy is welcome but we must be sure that the literacy learning provided for pre-school and reception children is appropriate.

Christopher Ball (1994) sets out the fundamental principles for good general practice in early years settings: children learn most effectively through actions rather than instruction and when they are actively involved and interested. It was obvious that Alice developed as a reader and writer not through direct instruction but through involvement with literacy, which she found to be interesting. Children in early years settings can also learn effectively in this manner without receiving constant direct instruction from adults or being required to use worksheets that are now being created for this age group. In the USA the International Reading Association (1998) has found it necessary to develop a statement of *Developmentally Appropriate Practices for Young Children* because they are so concerned that teaching practices suited to older children were being used inappropriately and ineffectively with children in pre-school, kindergarten and early grade class-rooms.

So what should be provided for young children in their early years classrooms? For Alice, as for the children observed in a *Bookstart* programme (Cooling, 1998), it was story readings which were most important. **Story readings** for individuals, groups and the class are a starting point also in early settings. Having more than one adult in the room allows readings to be held with one or two children at a time, as well as for the whole class. During story readings the children learn about how to handle books, starting at the beginning, and about using print to construct meaning (Strickland and Morrow, 1989). They also learn about new words, sentences and how stories are constructed (Dombey, 1988). In classrooms where the adults encourage the children to be actively involved in story readings, such learning is facilitated. Elsewhere I have provided examples of the interactive nature of such story readings and quoted the children's comments indicating their level of involvement and learning (Campbell, 1996).

How story readings can provide the basis for a whole range of activities, including painting, attempts at writing, story retellings, constructional activities and as a basis for play is described in greater detail by Ruby Campbell (1998), in her account of a day of literacy learning in a nursery classroom. From story readings the children learn not only about literacy but also about relationships, behaviour and a wider environment. Her account records that there was more than one reading of a story, because **rereading** benefits the children's literacy, as reported by Morrow (1988). When teachers repeat enjoyable story readings of worthwhile books, they extend the children's understanding of the story and enable the children to engage with the book on their own.

When a story is being read to the whole class, not all the children see the pictures, and more particularly the print, as clearly as they do at home with an adult. Consequently, Don Holdaway (1979) suggested that **big books** be used in a **shared book experience**, whether these be purchased or made in the classroom with the children. Shared book experiences in nursery settings can be much like the interactive story readings described in the present study. The adult reader can run a finger under each word as each is read, so that the notion of print as conveying meaning gets across to the children. It also gives children the chance to recognise particular words of interest to them – Alice, for instance, was interested in the word 'and' because it was the link word she needed when she tried to write 'Alice and Caitlin'. Children will connect with whichever words are of importance or interest to them.

At home, Alice had a shelf on which she knew she would find books she would enjoy. That is replicated and extended in early years class-rooms, where a **library corner** is an important feature, to which the children are attracted by carefully selected books. Teachers make reading corners inviting, with a carpet, chairs, displays of books, posters, and puppets and toys relating to the stories. All this en-courages the children towards books, as does the occasional visit by an adult to read aloud to the children who want to share a story. Even when no adult is present, two or three children are likely to be found in the library corner, reading or looking at books.

As the children move through pre-school towards the reception class some teachers set aside a time for **sustained silent reading**, when all the children read or demonstrate reading-like behaviours with a favourite book. During this specified time the adults can model silent reading by quietly reading their own books.

There are many opportunities for reading in a natural way. As Alice demonstrated, young children learn to read the signs and signals of **environmental print**, and adults can foster the children's interest in the print around them in the classroom. Miller (1998) suggests a wide range of activities suited to early years settings, such as making charts with favourite logos, creating 'I can read charts' of logos, or having a print party where the children wear clothing covered with prominent print. Labels and signs will already be part of **classroom print** but it is important for the teacher to make good use of them by reading the words to the children and talking about them. This then becomes another form of sharing print, whether it is charts of rhymes and key words, messages, weather charts, birthday lists or rules.

In addition to activities involving reading and a print-rich environment, young children need to be given constant **opportunities for writing**. A starting point can be providing resources for writing to support the children's **socio-dramatic play** (Hall and Robinson, 1995b) – a message pad and pencil next to the telephone allows children to write down messages after their imaginary telephone calls. The play area or home corner can variously be made into a post office, a dentist's rooms, a travel agency, a corner store and so on and will need directories, books, brochures, message pads, appointment charts, typewriters, computers etc., that will encourage children to engage purposefully with writing as well as reading.

Some settings provide a separate **writing table** holding various shapes of paper, pencils and other writing tools, so that the children can write shopping lists, create stories, make books, produce notices, and write cards. All this is supported with careful and sensitive support, modelling of writing and guidance from the adults. The younger children will make marks rather than producing relatively clear writing but others will produce writing with invented spellings (Graves, 1983) such as Alice did. Using invented, developmental or phonic spellings helps the children to explore letters and sounds and develop a base of understanding to support their later development.

One feature of the children's writing will be their attempts, from a young age, to **write their own names**. From about two and a half, Alice showed a sustained interest in producing her own name and this became a major aspect of her writing around her third birthday. Attention to one's own name is common, as other studies (e.g. Payton, 1984; Martens, 1986) confirm. In early years settings the adults can capitalise on that interest by encouraging the children to recognise their own names each day when they arrive, at break times, on their clothes pegs etc and to write their names on shopping lists, paintings and drawings and at so on. As Davies (1988) argued, attention to their own names encourages children to think about letters and their sequencing and so is an avenue to literacy. Some settings create a wall chart of all the children's names, in alphabetic order. Other key words can be added, to create a simple classroom dictionary and a valuable addition to the classroom print.

The wall dictionary, in alphabetic order, provides a reminder to children of the letters of the alphabet. Having **alphabetic knowledge** at five years of age is a good predictor of later reading success (Riley, 1996), but it is because the children have acquired this through a wide range of literacy events that this is so. The children have a foundation of literacy knowledge that underpins the alphabetic. Being taught the letters directly at age five is not the same as learning about them through a range of different experiences (Moustafa, 1997).

Younger children learn about letters in **alphabet songs**, and this generally helps them with the alphabet sequence too. Young children enjoy singing **nursery rhymes and songs**, and the words can be written by an adult in front of, and with, the children and then displayed as a big classroom poster and followed as the children sing. While singing, the children learn incidentally about features of words such as the onset and rime elements in, for instance, w-all and f-all in Humpty Dumpty. As Goswami and Bryant (1990) suggest, this will also support children's reading development.

This concluding chapter has indicated what early years educators might learn from Alice. This is not the place to go into great detail about the literacy provision in early years settings – it is already documented (Campbell, 1995 and 1996). The point here is that in early years classrooms children need to have many opportunities to engage with readily available print resources, to read, listen to stories, write and have the attention and encouragement they need from an adult when they approach a literacy activity. Each child should be given opportunities daily to experience meaningful and interesting reading and writing. Alice benefited immeasurably from the availability of worthwhile literacy resources and the constant support of adults when she set out to read and write at home each day, and children should have the benefit of similar experiences in their educational settings.

Bibliography

Ashton-Warner, S. (1963) *Teacher*. London: Secker and Warburg

Baghban, M. (1984) *Our Daughter Learns to Read and Write: A case study from birth to three*. Newark, DE: International Reading Association

Ball, C. (1994) *Start Right: The importance of early learning*. London: RSA

Bennett, J. (1991) 4th revised edition. *Learning to Read with Picture Books*. Stroud: The Thimble Press

Bissex, G. (1980) *Gnys at Wrk: A Child Learns to Read and Write*. Cambridge, Mass: Harvard Univ. Press

Campbell, R. (1993) *Miscue Analysis in the Classroom*. Shepreth, Herts: United Kingdom Reading Association

Campbell, R. (1995) *Reading in the Early Years Handbook*. Buckingham: Open University Press

Campbell, R. (1996) *Literacy in Nursery Education*. Stoke on Trent: Trentham Books

Campbell, R. E. (1998) A day of literacy learning in a nursery classroom. In R. Campbell (Ed) (1998) *Facilitating Literacy*. Newark, DE: International Reading Association

Chukovsky, K. (1963) *From Two to Five*. Berkeley: University of California Press

Clark, M. (1976) *Young Fluent Readers*. London: Heinemann Educational

Clay, M. (1972) *Reading: The Patterning of Complex Behaviour*. London: Heinemann Educational

Cooling, W. (1998) Get them booked up early. *Guardian Education*. 15.9.98. pp 4-5

Davies, A (1988) *Children's Names: Bridges to Literacy? Research in Education*. 40. pp 19-31

DfEE (1998) *The National Literacy Strategy*. London: Department for Education and Employment

Doake, D. (1988) *Reading Begins at Birth*. Richmond Hill, Ontario: Scholastic

Dombey, H. (1988) Partners in the telling. In M. Meek and C. Mills (Eds) *Language and Literacy in the Primary School*. Lewes: Falmer Press

Fox, C. (1993) *At the Very Edge of the Forest: The Influence of Literature on Storytelling by Children*. London: Cassell

Goddard, N. (1974) *Literacy: Language Experience Approach*. London: Macmillan Educational

Goodman, Y., Watson, D. and Burke, C. (1987) *Reading Miscue Inventory: Alternative Procedures*. New York: Richard C. Owen Publishers Inc

Goodman, Y. (Ed) (1990) *How Children Construct Literacy*. Newark, DE: International Reading Association

Graves, D. (1983) *WRITING: Teachers and Children at Work*. Portsmouth, New Hampshire: Heinemann

Goswami, U. C. and Bryant, P. (1990) *Phonological Skills and Learning to Read*. Hove: Lawrence Erlbaum Associates

Hall, N. and Robinson, A. (1995) *Looking at Literacy: Using images literacy to explore the world of reading and writing*. London: David Fulton

Hall, N. and Robinson, A. (1995b) *Exploring Writing and Play in the Early Years*. London: David Fulton

Hall, N. and Robinson, A. (1996) *Learning About Punctuation*. Clevedon: Multilingual Matters

Holdaway, D. (1979) *The Foundations of Literacy*. London: Ashton Scholastic

International Reading Association (1998) *Learning to Read and Write: Developmentally Appropriate Practices for Young Children*. Reprinted in *The Reading Teacher* 52.2. pp 193-216

Laminack, L. L. (1991) *Learning with Zachary*. Richmond Hill, Ontario: Scholastic

Marek, A. (1991) Retrospective Miscue Analysis: An instructional strategy for revaluing the reading process. In Goodman, K., Bird, L. and Goodman, Y. (1991) *The Whole Language Catalog*. Santa Rosa, Calif: American School Publishers

Martens, P (1996) *I Already Know How to Read: A Child's View of Literacy*. Portsmouth, New Hampshire: Heinemann

Meek, M. (1990) What do we know about reading that helps us to teach? In R. Carter (ed.), *Knowledge about Language and the Curriculum*. London: Hodder and Stoughton

Miller, L. (1998) *Moving towards literacy with environmental print*. Royston: United Kingdom Reading Association

Morrow, L. M. (1988) Young children's responses to one-to-one story readings in school settings. *Reading Research Quarterly*. 23.1. pp 89-107

Moustafa, M (1997) *Beyond Traditional Phonics: Research Discoveries and Reading Instruction*. Portsmouth, New Hampshire: Heinemann

Ninio, A and Bruner, H. (1978) The achievement and antecedents of labelling. *Journal of Child Language*. 5, 1-16

Opie, I and Opie, P. (1959) *The Lore and Language of School Children*. Oxford: Oxford University Press

Payton, S. (1984) Developing Awareness of Print: a young child's first steps towards literacy. Birmingham: *Educational Review*, University of Birmingham

Riley, J. (1996) The ability to label the letters of the alphabet at school entry: a discussion on its value. *Journal of Research in Reading*. 19.2 pp 87-101

SCAA (1996) *Nursery Education: Desirable Outcomes for Children's Learning*. London: Department for Education and Employment with School Curriculum and Assessment Authority

SCAA (1996) *Baseline Assessment scales*. London: School Curriculum and Assessment Authority

Shickedanz, J. A. (1990) *Adam's Righting Revolutions*. Portsmouth, New Hampshire: Heinemann

Spreadbury, J. (1994) *Read Me A Story: Parents, teachers and children as partners in literacy learning*. Carlton, Victoria: Australian Reading Association

Strickland, D. S. and Morrow, L. M. (Eds) (1989) *Emerging Literacy: Young Children Learn to Read and Write*. Newark, DE: International Reading Association.

Taylor, D. (1983) *Family Literacy: Young Children Learning to Read and Write*. Portsmouth, New Hampshire: Heinemann

Torrey, J. (1969) Learning to read without a teacher: a case study. *Elementary English*. 46. pp550-556

Trelease, J. (1989) *The New Read-Aloud Handbook* (2nd revised edition). New York: Penguin Books

Wells, G. (1986) *The Meaning Makers: Children Learning Language and Using Language to Learn*. London: Hodder and Stoughton

White, D. (1954) *Books Before Five*. Portsmouth, New Hampshire: Heinemann

Wolf, S. A. and Heath, S. B. (1992) *The Braid of Literature: Children's Worlds of Reading*. Cambridge, Mass: Harvard University Press

Children's books

Adamson, J. and Adamson, G. (1992) *Topsy and Tim ride their bikes.* London: Blackie

Adamson, J. and Adamson, G. (1996) *Topsy and Tim meet the ambulance crew.* Harmondsworth: Penguin

Adamson, J. and Adamson, G. (1997) *Topsy and Tim at the Sea Life Centre.* Harmondsworth: Penguin

BBC (1996) *Toybox – Bumper Story Book.* London: BBC Children's Books

Biro, V. (1995) *Jasper's Jungle Journey.* Loughborough: Ladybird

Bond, M. (1992) *Paddington has a Bath.* London: Harper Collins

Bond, M. (1992b) *Paddington Goes Shopping.* London: Harper Collins

Bond, M. (1992c) *Paddington at the Seaside.* London: Harper Collins

Briggs, R. (1994) *The Snowman.* Harmondsworth: Penguin

Burningham, J. (1970) *Mr Gumpy's Outing.* London: Jonathan Cape

Butterfield, M. (1995) *Zoo Animals.* Loughborough: Ladybird

Campbell, Rod. (1982) *Dear Zoo.* Harmondsworth: Penguin

Campbell, Rod. (1983) *Oh Dear!* London: Blackie and Son

Carle, E. (1969) *The Very Hungry Caterpillar.* London: Hamish Hamilton

Carle, E. (1988) *Do You Want to Be My Friend?* Boston: Houghton Mifflin

Carle, E. (1995) *The Very Lonely Firefly.* London: Hamish Hamilton

Disney, W. (1990) *Bambi.* Loughborough: Ladybird Books

Disney, W. (1993) *Jungle Book.* Loughborough: Ladybird Books

Dodd, L. (1983) *Hairy Maclary from Donaldson's Dairy.* Harmondsworth: Puffin

Dodd, L. (1984) *Hairy Maclary's Bone.* Harmondsworth: Puffin

Dodd, L. (1993) *Slinky Malinki, Open the door.* Harmondsworth: Puffin

Dodd, L. (1995) *Sniff – Snuff – Snap!* Harmondsworth: Puffin

Dudko, M. A. and Larsen, M. (1994) *A Day with Barney.* London: Viking

Early Learning Centre (n.d.) *Alphabet Frieze.* Swindon: Early Learning Centre

Early Learning Centre (n.d.) *My Favourite Things.* Swindon: Early Learning Centre

Early Learning Centre (1995) *50 Favourite Nursery Rhymes and Songs* (A CD recording) Harlow: CYP Ltd

Fox, M. (1988) *Koala Lou.* New York: A Voyager Book, Harcourt Brace

Ginn New Reading Level 2. (1993) *I can hide.* Aylesbury, Bucks: Ginn

Hawkins, C and Hawkins, J. (1987) *Here's a Happy Pig.* London: Walker Books

Hellen, N. (1988) *The Bus Stop.* London: Aurum Books for Children

Hill, Eric. (1966) *Spot's first words*. London: Heinemann

Hill, Eric. (1986) *Spot looks at colours*. London: Heinemann

Hill, Eric. (1991) *Spot's toy box*. London: Heinemann

Hughes, S. (1981) *Alfie Gets in First*. London: The Bodley Head

Hunia, F. (1993) *Sly Fox and Red Hen*. Loughborough: Ladybird

Hutchins, P. (1972) *Good-Night Owl*. London: The Bodley Head

Inkpen, M. (1991) *Kipper*. Sevenoaks: Hodder and Stoughton

Kemp, Moira. (Illustrator) (1990) *Hickory, Dickory, Dock*. Hemel Hempstead: Simon and Schuster Young Books

Kearns, K. and O'Brien, M. (1993) *Barney's Farm Animals*. London: Viking

Lindsay, W. (1991) *The Great Dinosaur Atlas*. London: Dorling Kindersley

Lyons, Sara. (1986) *Big Animals*. London: Walker Books

Mark, J. (1997) *Fur*. London: Walker Books

Matterson, E. (1969) *This Little Puffin ... Finger Plays and Nursery Games*. London: Puffin

Matthes, D. and Watson, B. (1986) *Animal Friends*. England: Brown Watson

Matthes, D. and Watson, B. (1986b) *Forest Friends*. England: Brown Watson

McKee, D. (1989) *Elmer the Patchwork Elephant*. London: Andersen

Murphy, J. (1995) *The Last Noo-Noo*. London: Walker Books

(n.d.) Nursery Rhymes – 1. Holland Enterprises Ltd

Oakley, H. (1988) *fire!* Aylesbury, Bucks: Ginn, Reading 360 Little Books

O'Neill, R. (1990) *Baby Owl*. London: Victoria House Publishing

Oxenbury, H. (1993) *It's My Birthday*. London: Walker Books

Pillinger, I. (n.d.) *Tuffy the Jeep*. Bridlington: Peter Haddock

Ragdoll Productions (1995) *Rosie and Jim: Going for a Walk*. London: Scholastic

Rayner, S. (1995) *Hey Diddle Diddle and other Mother Goose Rhymes*. Harmondsworth: Penguin

Ricken, N. (1990) *Baby's Colors*. New York: Simon and Schuster

Roffey, M. (1993) *Ten Little Teddy Bears*. Harmondsworth: Penguin

Seuss, Dr. (1960) *Green Eggs and Ham*. New York: Random House

Seuss, Dr. (1963) *Hop on Pop*. New York: Random House

Spurgeon, M. (1994) *Jungle Friends*. England: Brown Watson

Teeney Books Ltd (1991) *Duck's Friends on the Pond*. Frome, Somerset: Teeney Books

Teeney Books Ltd (1991) *Panda's Friends at the Zoo*. Frome, Somerset: Teeney Books

Tucker, Sian. (1990) *My Toys*. London: Orchard Books

Tyler, J. and Hawthorn, P. (1996) *There's a Monster in My House*. London: Usborne

VTECH (n.d.) *Talking Whiz Kid Power Mouse*. Abingdon, Oxon: VTECH

Waddell, M. (1989) *The Park in the Dark*. London: Walker Books

Wilhelm, H. (1988) *Tyrone the horrible*. London: Scholastic Hippo

Young, R. (1994) *Who Says Moo?* New York: Viking, Penguin

Young, S. (1994) *We're Not Tired*. London: Mammoth

Zinnemann-Hope, P. (1986) *Time for bed NED*. London: Walker Books